LSD

MY PROBLEM CHILD

LSD
MY PROBLEM CHILD
REFLECTIONS ON SACRED DRUGS, MYSTICISM, AND SCIENCE

ALBERT HOFMANN

Ph.D., Dr. Pharm. (Hon.), Dr. Sc. Nat. (Hon.)
Head of the Pharmaceutical-Chemical Research Laboratories,
Division of Natural Products (Retired), Sandoz, Ltd.,
Basel, Switzerland

Translated by Jonathan Ott

J. P. TARCHER, INC.
Los Angeles
Distributed by Houghton Mifflin Company
Boston

This work was first published in German in 1979 as *LSD—Mein Sorgenkind*.

Library of Congress Cataloging in Publication Data

Hofmann, Albert, 1906–
  LSD, my problem child.

     Translation of LSD, mein Sorgenkind.
  1. Lysergic acid diethylamide—History.
2. Psychobiology.   3. Mind and body.   4. Hofmann,
Albert, 1906–   I. Title.
BF209.L9H6313   615'.7883'0924 [B]   80-14536
ISBN 0-87477-256-7

J. P. Tarcher, Inc.
9110 Sunset Blvd.
Los Angeles, CA 90069

MANUFACTURED IN THE UNITED STATES OF AMERICA

D 10 9 8 7 6 5 4 3 2 1

Contents

Translator's Preface

Numerous accounts of the discovery of LSD have been published in English; none, unfortunately, have been completely accurate. Here, at last, the father of LSD details the history of his "problem child" and his long and fruitful career as a research chemist. In a real sense, this book is the inside story of the birth of the Psychedelic Age, and it cannot be denied that we have here a highly candid and personal insight into one of the most important scientific discoveries of our time, the significance of which has yet to dawn on mankind.

Surpassing its historical value is the immense philosophical import of this work. Never before has a chemist, an expert in the most materialistic of the sciences, advanced a *Weltanschauung* of such a mystical and transcendental nature. LSD, psilocybin, and the other hallucinogens do indeed, as Albert Hofmann asserts, constitute "cracks" in the edifice of materialistic rationality, cracks we would do well to explore and perhaps widen.

As a writer, it gives me great satisfaction to know that by this book the American reader interested in hallucinogens will be introduced to the work of Rudolf Gelpke, Ernst Jünger, and Walter Vogt, writers who are all but unknown here. With the notable exceptions of Huxley and Wasson, English and American writers on the hallucinogenic experience have been far less distinguished and eloquent than they.

This translation has been carefully overseen by Albert Hofmann, which made my task both simpler and more enjoyable. I am beholden to R. Gordon Wasson for checking the chapters on LSD's "Mexican relatives" and on "Ska María Pastora" for accuracy and style.

Two chapters of this book—"How LSD Originated" and "LSD Experience and Reality"—were presented by Albert Hofmann as a paper before the international conference "Hallucinogens, Shamanism and Modern Life" in San Francisco on the afternoon of Saturday, September 30, 1978. As a part of the conference proceedings, the first chapter has been published in the *Journal of Psychedelic Drugs*, Vol. 11 (1–2), 1979.

JONATHAN OTT
Vashon Island, Washington

FOREWORD

There are experiences that most of us are hesitant to speak about, because they do not conform to everyday reality and defy rational explanation. These are not particular external occurrences, but rather events of our inner lives, which are generally dismissed as figments of the imagination and barred from our memory. Suddenly, the familiar view of our surroundings is transformed in a strange, delightful, or alarming way: it appears to us in a new light, takes on a special meaning. Such an experience can be as light and fleeting as a breath of air, or it can imprint itself deeply upon our minds.

One enchantment of that kind, which I experienced in childhood, has remained remarkably vivid in my memory ever since. It happened on a May morning—I have forgotten the year—but I can still point to the exact spot where it occurred, on a forest path on Martinsberg above Baden, Switzerland. As I strolled through the freshly greened woods filled with bird song and lit up by the morning sun, all at once everything appeared in an uncommonly clear light. Was this something I had simply failed to notice before? Was I suddenly discovering the spring forest as it actually looked? It shone with the most beautiful radiance, speaking to the heart, as though it wanted to encompass me in its majesty. I was filled with an indescribable sensation of joy, oneness, and blissful security.

I have no idea how long I stood there spellbound. But I recall the anxious concern I felt as the radiance slowly dissolved and I hiked on: how could a vision that was so real and convincing, so directly and deeply felt—how could it end so soon? And how could I tell anyone about it, as my overflowing joy compelled me to do, since I knew there were no words to describe what I had seen? It seemed strange that I, as a child, had seen something so marvelous, something that adults obviously did not perceive—for I had never heard them mention it.

While still a child, I experienced several more of these deeply euphoric moments on my rambles through forest and meadow. It was these experiences that shaped the main outlines of my world view and convinced me of the existence of a miraculous, powerful, unfathomable reality that was hidden from everyday sight.

I was often troubled in those days, wondering if I would ever, as an adult, be able to communicate these experiences; whether I would have the chance to depict my visions in poetry or paintings. But knowing that I was not cut out to be a poet or artist, I assumed I would have to keep these experiences to myself, important as they were to me.

Unexpectedly—though scarcely by chance—much later, in middle age, a link was established between my profession and these visionary experiences from childhood.

Because I wanted to gain insight into the structure and essence of matter, I became a research chemist.

Intrigued by the plant world since early childhood, I chose to specialize in research on the constituents of medicinal plants. In the course of this career I was led to the psychoactive, hallucination-causing substances, which under certain conditions can evoke visionary states similar to the spontaneous experiences just described. The most important of these hallucinogenic substances has come to be known as LSD. Hallucinogens, as active compounds of considerable scientific interest, have gained entry into medicinal research, biology, and psychiatry, and later—especially LSD—also obtained wide diffusion in the drug culture.

In studying the literature connected with my work, I became aware of the great universal significance of visionary experience. It plays a dominant role, not only in mysticism and the history of religion, but also in the creative process in art, literature, and science. More recent investigations have shown that many persons also have visionary experiences in daily life, though most of us fail to recognize their meaning and value. Mystical experiences, like those that marked my childhood, are apparently far from rare.

There is today a widespread striving for mystical experience, for visionary breakthroughs to a deeper, more comprehensive reality than that perceived by our rational, everyday consciousness. Efforts to transcend our materialistic world view are being made in various ways, not only by the adherents to Eastern religious movements, but also by professional psychiatrists, who are adopting such profound spiritual experiences as a basic therapeutic principle.

I share the belief of many of my contemporaries that the spiritual crisis pervading all spheres of Western industrial society can be remedied only by a change in our world view. We shall have to shift from the materialistic, dualistic belief that people and their environment are separate, toward a new consciousness of an all-encompassing reality, which embraces the experiencing ego, a reality in which people feel their oneness with animate nature and all of creation.

Everything that can contribute to such a fundamental alteration in our perception of reality must therefore command earnest attention. Foremost among such approaches are the various methods of meditation, either in a religious or a secular context, which aim to deepen the consciousness of reality by way of a total mystical experience. Another important, but still controversial, path to the same goal is the use of the consciousness-altering properties of hallucinogenic psychopharmaceuticals. LSD finds such an application in medicine, by helping patients in psychoanalysis and psychotherapy to perceive their problems in their true significance.

Deliberate provocation of mystical experience, particularly by LSD and related hallucinogens, in contrast to spontaneous visionary experiences, entails dangers that must not be underestimated. Practitioners must take into account the peculiar effects of these substances, namely their ability to influence our consciousness, the innermost essence of our being. The history of LSD to date amply demonstrates the catastrophic consequences that can ensue when its profound effect is misjudged and the substance is mistaken for a pleasure drug. Special internal and external advance preparations are required; with them, an LSD experiment can become a meaningful experience. Wrong and inappropriate use has caused LSD to become my problem child.

It is my desire in this book to give a comprehensive picture of LSD, its origin, its effects, and its dangers, in order to guard against increasing abuse of this extraordinary drug. I hope thereby to emphasize possible uses of LSD that are compatible with its characteristic action. I believe that if people would learn to use LSD's vision-inducing capability more wisely, under suitable conditions, in medical practice and in conjunction with meditation, then in the future this problem child could become a wonder child.

1

How LSD Originated

*In the realm of scientific observation, luck
is granted only to those who are prepared.*
Louis Pasteur

Time and again I hear or read that LSD was discovered
by accident. This is only partly true. LSD came into
being within a systematic research program, and the
"accident" did not occur until much later: when LSD
was already five years old, I happened to experience its
unforeseeable effects in my own body—or rather, in
my own mind.

Looking back over my professional career to trace
the influential events and decisions that eventually
steered my work toward the synthesis of LSD, I realize
that the most decisive step was my choice of employment upon completion of my chemistry studies. If that
decision had been different, then this substance,
which has become known the world over, might never
have been created. In order to tell the story of the

1

origin of LSD, then, I must also touch briefly on my career as a chemist, since the two developments are inextricably interrelated.

In the spring of 1929, on concluding my chemistry studies at the University of Zürich, I joined the Sandoz Company's pharmaceutical-chemical research laboratory in Basel, as a co-worker with Professor Arthur Stoll, founder and director of the pharmaceutical department. I chose this position because it afforded me the opportunity to work on natural products, whereas two other job offers from chemical firms in Basel had involved work in the field of synthetic chemistry.

First Chemical Explorations

My doctoral work at Zürich under Professor Paul Karrer had already given me one chance to pursue my interest in plant and animal chemistry. Making use of the gastrointestinal juice of the vineyard snail, I accomplished the enzymatic degradation of chitin, the structural material of which the shells, wings, and claws of insects, crustaceans, and other lower animals are composed. I was able to derive the chemical structure of chitin from the cleavage product, a nitrogen-containing sugar, obtained by this degradation. Chitin turned out to be an analogue of cellulose, the structural material of plants. This important result, obtained after only three months of research, led to a doctoral thesis rated "with distinction."

When I joined the Sandoz firm, the staff of the pharmaceutical-chemical department was still rather modest in number. Four chemists with doctoral degrees worked in research, three in production.

In Stoll's laboratory I found employment that completely agreed with me as a research chemist. The objective that Professor Stoll had set for his pharmaceutical-chemical research laboratories was to isolate the active principles (i.e., the effective constituents) of known medicinal plants to produce pure specimens of these substances. This is particularly important in the case of medicinal plants whose active principles are unstable, or whose potency is subject to great variation, which makes an exact dosage difficult. But if the active principle is available in pure form, it becomes possible to manufacture a stable pharmaceutical preparation, exactly quantifiable by weight. With this in mind, Professor Stoll had elected to study plant substances of recognized value such as the substances from foxglove (*Digitalis*), Mediterranean squill (*Scilla maritima*), and ergot of rye (*Claviceps purpurea* or *Secale cornutum*), which, owing to their instability and uncertain dosage, nevertheless, had been little used in medicine.

My first years in the Sandoz laboratories were devoted almost exclusively to studying the active principles of Mediterranean squill. Dr. Walter Kreis, one of Professor Stoll's earliest associates, launched me in this field of research. The most important constituents of Mediterranean squill already existed in pure form. Their active agents, as well as those of woolly foxglove (*Digitalis lanata*), had been isolated and purified, chiefly by Dr. Kreis, with extraordinary skill.

The active principles of Mediterranean squill belong to the group of cardioactive glycosides (glycoside = sugar-containing substance) and serve, as do those of foxglove, in the treatment of cardiac insufficiency. The cardiac glycosides are extremely active substances. Because the therapeutic and the toxic doses differ so little, it becomes especially important here to have an exact dosage, based on pure compounds.

3

At the beginning of my investigations, a pharmaceutical preparation with *Scilla* glycosides had already been introduced into therapeutics by Sandoz; however, the chemical structure of these active compounds, with the exception of the sugar portion, remained largely unknown.

My main contribution to the *Scilla* research, in which I participated with enthusiasm, was to elucidate the chemical structure of the common nucleus of *Scilla* glycosides, showing on the one hand their differences from the *Digitalis* glycosides, and on the other hand their close structural relationship with the toxic principles isolated from skin glands of toads. In 1935, these studies were temporarily concluded.

Looking for a new field of research, I asked Professor Stoll to let me continue the investigations on the alkaloids of ergot, which he had begun in 1917 and which had led directly to the isolation of ergotamine in 1918. Ergotamine, discovered by Stoll, was the first ergot alkaloid obtained in pure chemical form. Although ergotamine quickly took a significant place in therapeutics (under the trade name Gynergen) as a hemostatic remedy in obstetrics and as a medicament in the treatment of migraine, chemical research on ergot in the Sandoz laboratories was abandoned after the isolation of ergotamine and the determination of its empirical formula. Meanwhile, at the beginning of the thirties, English and American laboratories had begun to determine the chemical structure of ergot alkaloids. They had also discovered a new, water-soluble ergot alkaloid, which could likewise be isolated from the mother liquor of ergotamine production. So I thought it was high time that Sandoz resumed chemical research on ergot alkaloids, unless we wanted to risk losing our leading role in a field of medicinal research, which was already becoming so important.

Professor Stoll granted my request, with some misgivings: "I must warn you of the difficulties you face in working with ergot alkaloids. These are exceedingly sensitive, easily decomposed substances, less stable than any of the compounds you have investigated in the cardiac glycoside field. But you are welcome to try."

And so the switches were thrown, and I found myself engaged in a field of study that would become the main theme of my professional career. I have never forgotten the creative joy, the eager anticipation I felt in embarking on the study of ergot alkaloids, at that time a relatively uncharted field of research.

Ergot

It may be helpful here to give some background information about ergot itself.* It is produced by a lower fungus (*Claviceps purpurea*) that grows parasitically on rye and, to a lesser extent, on other species of grain and on wild grasses. Kernels infested with this fungus develop into light-brown to violet-brown curved pegs (sclerotia) that push forth from the husk in place of normal grains. Ergot is described botanically as a sclerotium, the form that the ergot fungus takes in winter. Ergot of rye (*Secale cornutum*) is the variety used medicinally.

*For further information on ergot, readers should refer to the monographs of G. Barger, *Ergot and Ergotism* (Gurney and Jackson, London, 1931) and A. Hofmann, *Die Mutterkornalkaloide* (F. Enke Verlag, Stuttgart, 1964). The former is a classical presentation of the history of the drug, while the latter emphasizes the chemical aspects.

Ergot, more than any other drug, has a fascinating history, in the course of which its role and meaning have been reversed: once dreaded as a poison, in the course of time it has changed to a rich storehouse of valuable remedies. Ergot first appeared on the stage of history in the early Middle Ages, as the cause of outbreaks of mass poisonings affecting thousands of persons at a time. The illness, whose connection with ergot was for a long time obscure, appeared in two characteristic forms, one gangrenous (*ergotismus gangraenosus*) and the other convulsive (*ergotismus convulsivus*). Popular names for ergotism—such as "mal des ardents," "ignis sacer," "heiliges Feuer," or "St. Anthony's fire"—refer to the gangrenous form of the disease. The patron saint of ergotism victims was St. Anthony, and it was primarily the Order of St. Anthony that treated these patients.

Until recent times, epidemic-like outbreaks of ergot poisoning have been recorded in most European countries including certain areas of Russia. With progress in agriculture, and since the realization, in the seventeenth century, that ergot-containing bread was the cause, the frequency and extent of ergotism epidemics diminished considerably. The last great epidemic occurred in certain areas of southern Russia in the years 1926–27.*

The first mention of a medicinal use of ergot, namely as an ecbolic (a medicament to precipitate childbirth), is found in the herbal of the Frankfurt city physician Adam Lonitzer (Lonicerus) in the year 1582. Although ergot, as Lonitzer stated, had been used since olden times by midwives, it was not until 1808 that this drug

---

*The mass poisoning in the southern French city of Pont-St. Esprit in the year 1951, which many writers have attributed to ergot-containing bread, actually had nothing to do with ergotism. It rather involved poisoning by an organic mercury compound that was utilized for disinfecting seed.

gained entry into academic medicine, on the strength of a work by the American physician John Stearns entitled *Account of the Pulvis Parturiens, a Remedy for Quickening Childbirth*. The use of ergot as an ecbolic did not, however, endure. Practitioners became aware quite early of the great danger to the child, owing primarily to the uncertainty of dosage, which when too high led to uterine spasms. From then on, the use of ergot in obstetrics was confined to stopping postpartum hemorrhage (bleeding after childbirth).

It was not until ergot's recognition in various pharmacopoeias during the first half of the nineteenth century that the first steps were taken toward isolating the active principles of the drug. However, of all the researchers who assayed this problem during the first hundred years, not one succeeded in identifying the actual substances responsible for the therapeutic activity. In 1907, the Englishmen G. Barger and F. H. Carr were the first to isolate an active alkaloidal preparation, which they named ergotoxine because it produced more of the toxic than therapeutic properties of ergot. (This preparation was not homogeneous, but rather a mixture of several alkaloids, as I was able to show thirty-five years later.) Nevertheless, the pharmacologist H. H. Dale discovered that ergotoxine, besides the uterotonic effect, also had an antagonistic activity on adrenaline in the autonomic nervous system that could lead to the therapeutic use of ergot alkaloids. Only with the isolation of ergotamine by A. Stoll (as mentioned previously) did an ergot alkaloid find entry and widespread use in therapeutics.

The early 1930s brought a new era in ergot research, beginning with the determination of the chemical structure of ergot alkaloids, as mentioned, in English and American laboratories. By chemical cleavage, W. A. Jacobs and L. C. Craig of the Rockefeller Institute of New York succeeded in isolating and characterizing the nucleus common to all ergot alkaloids. They named it lysergic acid. Then came a major development, both for chemistry and for medicine: the isolation of the specifically uterotonic, hemostatic principle of ergot, which was published simultaneously and quite independently by four institutions, including the Sandoz laboratories. The substance, an alkaloid of comparatively simple structure, was named ergobasine (syn. ergometrine, ergonovine) by A. Stoll and E. Burckhardt. By the chemical degradation of ergobasine, W. A. Jacobs and L. C. Craig obtained lysergic acid and the amino alcohol propanolamine as cleavage products.

I set as my first goal the problem of preparing this alkaloid synthetically, through chemical linking of the two components of ergobasine, lysergic acid and propanolamine (see structural formulas in the appendix).

The lysergic acid necessary for these studies had to be obtained by chemical cleavage of some other ergot alkaloid. Since only ergotamine was available as a pure alkaloid, and was already being produced in kilogram quantities in the pharmaceutical production department, I chose this alkaloid as the starting material for my work. I set about obtaining 0.5 gm of ergotamine from the ergot production people. When I sent the internal requisition form to Professor Stoll for his countersignature, he appeared in my laboratory and reproved me: "If you want to work with ergot alkaloids, you will have to familiarize yourself with the techniques of microchemistry. I can't have you consuming such a large amount of my expensive ergotamine for your experiments."

The ergot production department, besides using ergot of Swiss origin to obtain ergotamine, also dealt with Portuguese ergot, which yielded an amorphous alkaloidal preparation that corresponded to the aforementioned ergotoxine first produced by Barger and Carr. I decided to use this less expensive material for the preparation of lysergic acid. The alkaloid obtained from the production department had to be purified further, before it would be suitable for cleavage to lysergic acid. Observations made during the purification process led me to think that ergotoxine could be a mixture of several alkaloids, rather than one homogeneous alkaloid. I will speak later of the far-reaching sequelae of these observations.

Here I must digress briefly to describe the working conditions and techniques that prevailed in those days. These remarks may be of interest to the present generation of research chemists in industry, who are accustomed to far better conditions.

We were very frugal. Individual laboratories were considered a rare extravagance. During the first six years of my employment with Sandoz, I shared a laboratory with two colleagues. We three chemists, plus an assistant each, worked in the same room on three different fields: Dr. Kreiss on cardiac glycosides; Dr. Wiedemann, who joined Sandoz around the same time as I, on the leaf pigment chlorophyll; and I ultimately on ergot alkaloids. The laboratory was equipped with two fume hoods (compartments supplied with outlets), providing less than effective ventilation by gas flames. When we requested that these hoods be equipped with ventilators, our chief refused on the gound that ventilation by gas flame had sufficed in Willstätter's laboratory.

During the last years of World War I, Professor Stoll had been an assistant in Berlin and Munich to the world-famous chemist and Nobel laureate Professor Richard Willstätter, and with him had conducted the fundamental investigations on chlorophyll and the assimilation of carbon dioxide. There was scarcely a scientific discussion with Professor Stoll in which he did not mention his revered teacher Professor Willstätter and his work in Willstätter's laboratory.

The working techniques available to chemists in the field of organic chemistry at that time (the beginning of the thirties) were essentially the same as those employed by Justus von Liebig a hundred years earlier. The most important development achieved since then was the introduction of microanalysis by B. Pregl, which made it possible to ascertain the elemental composition of a compound with only a few milligrams of specimen, whereas earlier a few centigrams were needed. Of the other physical-chemical techniques at the disposal of the chemist today—techniques which have changed his way of working, making it faster and more effective, and created entirely new possibilities, above all for the elucidation of structure—none yet existed in those days.

For the investigations of *Scilla* glycosides and the first studies in the ergot field, I still used the old separation and purification techniques from Liebig's day: fractional extraction, fractional precipitation, fractional crystallization, and the like. The introduction of column chromatography, the first important step in modern laboratory technique, was of great value to me only in later investigations. For structure determination, which today can be conducted rapidly and elegantly with the help of spectroscopic methods (UV, IR, NMR) and X-ray crystallography, we had to rely, in the first fundamental ergot studies, entirely on the old laborious methods of chemical degradation and derivatization.

Lysergic Acid and Its Derivatives

Lysergic acid proved to be a rather unstable substance, and its rebonding with basic radicals posed difficulties. In the technique known as Curtius' Synthesis, I ultimately found a process that proved useful for combining lysergic acid with amines. With this method I produced a great number of lysergic acid compounds. By combining lysergic acid with the amino alcohol propanolamine, I obtained a compound that was identical to the natural ergot alkaloid ergobasine. With that, the first synthesis—that is, artificial production—of an ergot alkaloid was accomplished. This was not only of scientific interest, as confirmation of the chemical structure of ergobasine, but also of practical significance, because ergobasine, the specifically uterotonic, hemostatic principle, is present in ergot only in very trifling quantities. With this synthesis, the other alkaloids existing abundantly in ergot could now be converted to ergobasine, which was valuable in obstetrics.

After this first success in the ergot field, my investigations went forward on two fronts. First, I attempted to improve the pharmacological properties of ergobasine by variations of its amino alcohol radical. My colleague Dr. J. Peyer and I developed a process for the economical production of propanolamine and other amino alcohols. Indeed, by substitution of the propanolamine contained in ergobasine with the amino alcohol butanolamine, an active principle was obtained that even surpassed the natural alkaloid in its therapeutic properties. This improved ergobasine has found worldwide application as a dependable uterotonic, hemostatic remedy under the trade name Methergine, and is today the leading medicament for this indication in obstetrics.

I further employed my synthetic procedure to produce new lysergic acid compounds for which uterotonic activity was not prominent, but from which, on the basis of their chemical structure, other types of interesting pharmacological properties could be expected. In 1938, I produced the twenty-fifth substance in this series of lysergic acid derivatives: lysergic acid diethylamide, abbreviated LSD-25 (Lysergsäure-diäthylamid) for laboratory usage.

I had planned the synthesis of this compound with the intention of obtaining a circulatory and respiratory stimulant (an analeptic). Such stimulating properties could be expected for lysergic acid diethylamide, because it shows similarity in chemical structure to the analeptic already known at that time, namely nicotinic acid diethylamide (Coramine). During the testing of LSD-25 in the pharmacological department of Sandoz, whose director at the time was Professor Ernst Rothlin, a strong effect on the uterus was established. It amounted to some 70 percent of the activity of ergobasine. The research report also noted, in passing, that the experimental animals became restless during the narcosis. The new substance, however, aroused no special interest in our pharmacologists and physicians; testing was therefore discontinued.

For the next five years, nothing more was heard of the substance LSD-25. Meanwhile, my work in the ergot field advanced further in other areas. Through the purification of ergotoxine, the starting material for lysergic acid, I obtained, as already mentioned, the impression that this alkaloidal preparation was not homogeneous, but was rather a mixture of different substances. This doubt as to the homogeneity of ergotoxine was reinforced when in its hydrogenation two distinctly different hydrogenation products were obtained, whereas the homogeneous alkaloid ergotamine under the same condition yielded only a single hydrogenation product (hydrogenation = introduction of hydrogen). Extended, systematic analytical investigations of the supposed ergotoxine mixture led ultimately to the separation of this alkaloidal preparation into three homogeneous components. One of the three chemically homogeneous ergotoxine alkaloids proved to be identical with an alkaloid isolated shortly before in the production department, which A. Stoll and E. Burckhardt had named ergocristine. The other two alkaloids were both new. The first I named ergocornine; and for the second, the last to be isolated, which had long remained hidden in the mother liquor, I chose the name ergokryptine (kryptos = hidden). Later it was found that ergokryptine occurs in two isomeric forms, which were differentiated as α- and β-ergokryptine.

The solution of the ergotoxine problem was not merely scientifically interesting, but also had great practical significance. A valuable remedy arose from it. The three hydrogenated ergotoxine alkaloids that I produced in the course of these investigations, dihydroergocristine, dihydroergokryptine, and dihydroergocornine, displayed medicinally useful properties during testing by Professor Rothlin in the pharmacological department. From these three substances, the pharmaceutical preparation Hydergine was developed, a medicament for improvement of peripheral circulation and cerebral function in the control of geriatric disorders. Hydergine has proven to be an effective remedy in geriatrics for these indications. Today it is Sandoz's most important pharmaceutical product.

Dihydroergotamine, which I likewise produced in the course of these investigations, has also found application in therapeutics as a circulation- and blood-pressure-stabilizing medicament, under the trade name Dihydergot.

While today research on important projects is almost exclusively carried out as teamwork, the investigations on ergot alkaloids described above were conducted by myself alone. Even the further chemical steps in the evolution of commercial preparations remained in my hands—that is, the preparation of larger specimens for the clinical trials, and finally the perfection of the first procedures for mass production of Methergine, Hydergine, and Dihydergot. This even included the analytical controls for the development of the first galenical forms of these three preparations: the ampules, liquid solutions, and tablets. My aides at that time included a laboratory assistant, a laboratory helper, and later in addition a second laboratory assistant and a chemical technician.

Discovery of the Psychic Effects of LSD

The solution of the ergotoxine problem had led to fruitful results, described here only briefly, and had opened up further avenues of research. And yet I could not forget the relatively uninteresting LSD-25. A peculiar presentiment—the feeling that this substance could possess properties other than those established in the first investigations—induced me, five years after the first synthesis, to produce LSD-25 once again so that a sample could be given to the pharmacological department for further tests. This was quite unusual; experimental substances, as a rule, were definitely stricken from the research program if once found to be lacking in pharmacological interest.

Nevertheless, in the spring of 1943, I repeated the synthesis of LSD-25. As in the first synthesis, this involved the production of only a few centigrams of the compound.

In the final step of the synthesis, during the purification and crystallization of lysergic acid diethylamide in the form of a tartrate (tartaric acid salt), I was interrupted in my work by unusual sensations. The following description of this incident comes from the report that I sent at the time to Professor Stoll:

> Last Friday, April 16, 1943, I was forced to interrupt my work in the laboratory in the middle of the afternoon and proceed home, being affected by a remarkable restlessness, combined with a slight dizziness. At home I lay down and sank into a not unpleasant intoxicated-like condition, characterized by an extremely stimulated imagination. In a dreamlike state, with eyes closed (I found the daylight to be unpleasantly glaring), I perceived an uninterrupted stream of fantastic pictures, extraordinary shapes with intense, kaleidoscopic play of colors. After some two hours this condition faded away.

This was, altogether, a remarkable experience—both in its sudden onset and its extraordinary course. It seemed to have resulted from some external toxic influence; I surmised a connection with the substance I had been working with at the time, lysergic acid diethylamide tartrate. But this led to another question: how had I managed to absorb this material? Because of the known toxicity of ergot substances, I always maintained meticulously neat work habits. Possibly a bit of the LSD solution had contacted my fingertips during crystallization, and a trace of the substance was absorbed through the skin. If LSD-25 had indeed been the cause of this bizarre experience, then it must be a substance of extraordinary potency. There seemed to be only one way of getting to the bottom of this. I decided on a self-experiment.

Exercising extreme caution, I began the planned series of experiments with the smallest quantity that could be expected to produce some effect, considering the activity of the ergot alkaloids known at the time: namely, 0.25 mg (mg = milligram = one thousandth of a gram) of lysergic acid diethylamide tartrate. Quoted below is the entry for this experiment in my laboratory journal of April 19, 1943.

Self-Experiments

4/19/43 16:20: 0.5 cc of ½ promil aqueous solution of diethylamide tartrate orally = 0.25 mg tartrate. Taken diluted with about 10 cc water. Tasteless.

17:00: Beginning dizziness, feeling of anxiety, visual distortions, symptoms of paralysis, desire to laugh.

Supplement of 4/21: Home by bicycle. From 18:00–ca. 20:00 most severe crisis. (See special report.)

Here the notes in my laboratory journal cease. I was able to write the last words only with great effort. By now it was already clear to me that LSD had been the cause of the remarkable experience of the previous Friday, for the altered perceptions were of the same type as before, only much more intense. I had to struggle to speak intelligibly. I asked my laboratory assistant, who was informed of the self-experiment, to escort me home. We went by bicycle, no automobile being available because of wartime restrictions on their use. On the way home, my condition began to assume threatening forms. Everything in my field of vision wavered and was distorted as if seen in a curved mirror. I also had the sensation of being unable to move from the spot. Nevertheless, my assistant later told me that we had traveled very rapidly. Finally, we arrived at home safe and sound, and I was just barely capable of asking my companion to summon our family doctor and request milk from the neighbors.

In spite of my delirious, bewildered condition, I had brief periods of clear and effective thinking—and chose milk as a nonspecific antidote for poisoning.

The dizziness and sensation of fainting became so strong at times that I could no longer hold myself erect, and had to lie down on a sofa. My surroundings had now transformed themselves in more terrifying ways. Everything in the room spun around, and the familiar objects and pieces of furniture assumed grotesque, threatening forms. They were in continuous motion, animated, as if driven by an inner restlessness. The lady next door, whom I scarcely recognized, brought me milk—in the course of the evening I drank more than two liters. She was no longer Mrs. R., but rather a malevolent, insidious witch with a colored mask.

Even worse than these demonic transformations of the outer world, were the alterations that I perceived in myself, in my inner being. Every exertion of my will, every attempt to put an end to the disintegration of the outer world and the dissolution of my ego, seemed to be wasted effort. A demon had invaded me, had taken possession of my body, mind, and soul. I jumped up and screamed, trying to free myself from him, but then

17

sank down again and lay helpless on the sofa. The substance, with which I had wanted to experiment, had vanquished me. It was the demon that scornfully triumphed over my will. I was seized by the dreadful fear of going insane. I was taken to another world, another place, another time. My body seemed to be without sensation, lifeless, strange. Was I dying? Was this the transition? At times I believed myself to be outside my body, and then perceived clearly, as an outside observer, the complete tragedy of my situation. I had not even taken leave of my family (my wife, with our three children had traveled that day to visit her parents, in Lucerne). Would they ever understand that I had not experimented thoughtlessly, irresponsibly, but rather with the utmost caution, and that such a result was in no way foreseeable? My fear and despair intensified, not only because a young family should lose its father, but also because I dreaded leaving my chemical research work, which meant so much to me, unfinished in the midst of fruitful, promising development. Another reflection took shape, an idea full of bitter irony: if I was now forced to leave this world prematurely, it was because of this lysergic acid diethylamide that I myself had brought forth into the world.

By the time the doctor arrived, the climax of my despondent condition had already passed. My laboratory assistant informed him about my self-experiment, as I myself was not yet able to formulate a coherent sentence. He shook his head in perplexity, after my attempts to describe the mortal danger that threatened my body. He could detect no abnormal symptoms other than extremely dilated pupils. Pulse, blood pressure, breathing were all normal. He saw no reason to prescribe any medication. Instead he conveyed me to my bed and stood watch over me. Slowly I came back from a weird, unfamiliar world to reassuring everyday reality. The horror softened and gave way to a feeling of good fortune and gratitude, the more normal perceptions and thoughts returned, and I became more confident that the danger of insanity was conclusively past.

Now, little by little I could begin to enjoy the unprecedented colors and plays of shapes that persisted behind my closed eyes. Kaleidoscopic, fantastic images surged in on me, alternating, variegated, opening and then closing themselves in circles and spirals, exploding in colored fountains, rearranging and hybridizing themselves in constant flux. It was particularly remarkable how every acoustic perception, such as the sound of a door handle or a passing automobile, became transformed into optical perceptions. Every sound generated a vividly changing image, with its own consistent form and color.

Late in the evening my wife returned from Lucerne. Someone had informed her by telephone that I was suffering a mysterious breakdown. She had returned home at once, leaving the children behind with her parents. By now, I had recovered myself sufficiently to tell her what had happened.

Exhausted, I then slept, to awake next morning refreshed, with a clear head, though still somewhat tired physically. A sensation of well-being and renewed life flowed through me. Breakfast tasted delicious and gave me extraordinary pleasure. When I later walked out into the garden, in which the sun shone now after a spring rain, everything glistened and sparkled in a fresh light. The world was as if newly created. All my senses vibrated in a condition of highest sensitivity, which persisted for the entire day.

This self-experiment showed that LSD-25 behaved as a psychoactive substance with extraordinary properties and potency. There was to my knowledge no other known substance that evoked such profound psychic effects in such extremely low doses, that caused such dramatic changes in human consciousness and our experience of the inner and outer world.

What seemed even more significant was that I could remember the experience of LSD inebriation in every detail. This could only mean that the conscious recording function was not interrupted, even in the climax of the LSD experience, despite the profound breakdown of the normal world view. For the entire duration of the experiment, I had even been aware of participating in an experiment, but despite this recognition of my condition, I could not, with every exertion of my will, shake off the LSD world. Everything was experienced as completely real, as alarming reality; alarming, because the picture of the other, familiar everyday reality was still fully preserved in the memory for comparison.

Another surprising aspect of LSD was its ability to produce such a far-reaching, powerful state of inebriation without leaving a hangover. Quite the contrary, on the day after the LSD experiment I felt myself to be, as already described, in excellent physical and mental condition.

I was aware that LSD, a new active compound with such properties, would have to be of use in pharmacology, in neurology, and especially in psychiatry, and that it would attract the interest of concerned specialists. But at that time I had no inkling that the new substance would also come to be used beyond medical science, as an inebriant in the drug scene. Since my self-experiment had revealed LSD in its terrifying, demonic aspect, the last thing I could have expected was that this substance could ever find application as anything approaching a pleasure drug. I failed, moreover, to recognize the meaningful connection between LSD inebriation and spontaneous visionary experience until much later, after further experiments, which were carried out with far lower doses and under different conditions.

The next day I wrote to Professor Stoll the above-mentioned report about my extraordinary experience with LSD-25 and sent a copy to the director of the pharmacological department, Professor Rothlin.

As expected, the first reaction was incredulous astonishment. Instantly a telephone call came from the management; Professor Stoll asked: "Are you certain you made no mistake in the weighing? Is the stated dose really correct?" Professor Rothlin also called, asking the same question. I was certain of this point, for I had executed the weighing and dosage with my own hands. Yet their doubts were justified to some extent, for until then no known substance had displayed even the slightest psychic effect in fraction-of-a-milligram doses. An active compound of such potency seemed almost unbelievable.

Professor Rothlin himself and two of his colleagues were the first to repeat my experiment, with only one-third of the dose I had utilized. But even at that level, the effects were still extremely impressive, and quite fantastic. All doubts about the statements in my report were eliminated.

2

LSD in Animal Experiments and Biological Research

After the discovery of its extraordinary psychic effects, the substance LSD-25, which five years earlier had been excluded from further investigation after the first trials on animals, was again admitted into the series of experimental preparations. Most of the fundamental studies on animals were carried out by Dr. Aurelio Cerletti in the Sandoz pharmacological department, headed by Professor Rothlin.

Before a new active substance can be investigated in systematic clinical trials with human subjects, extensive data on its effects and side effects must be determined in pharmacological tests on animals. These experiments must assay the assimilation and elimination of the particular substance in organisms, and above all its tolerance and relative toxicity. Only the most important reports on animal experiments with LSD, and those intelligible to the layperson, will be reviewed here. It would greatly exceed the scope of this book if I attempted to mention all the results of several hundred pharmacological investigations, which have been conducted all over the world in connection with the fundamental work on LSD in the Sandoz laboratories.

Animal experiments reveal little about the mental alterations caused by LSD because psychic effects are scarcely determinable in lower animals, and even in the more highly developed, they can be established only to a limited extent. LSD produces its effects above all in the sphere of the higher and highest psychic and intellectual functions. It is therefore understandable that specific reactions to LSD can be expected only in higher animals. Subtle psychic changes cannot be established in animals because, even if they should be occurring, the animal could not give them expression. Thus, only relatively heavy psychic disturbances, expressing themselves in the altered behavior of research animals, become discernible. Quantities that are substantially higher than the effective dose of LSD in human beings are therefore necessary, even in higher animals like cats, dogs, and apes.

While the mouse under LSD shows only motor disturbances and alterations in licking behavior, in the cat we see, besides vegetative symptoms like bristling of the hair (piloerection) and salivation, indications that point to the existence of hallucinations. The animals stare anxiously in the air, and instead of attacking the mouse, the cat leaves it alone or will even stand in fear before the mouse. One could also conclude that the behavior of dogs that are under the influence of LSD involves hallucinations. A caged community of chimpanzees reacts very sensitively if a member of the tribe has received LSD. Even though no changes appear in this single animal, the whole cage gets in an uproar because the LSD chimpanzee no longer observes the laws of its finely coordinated hierarchic tribal order.

Of the remaining animal species on which LSD was tested, only aquarium fish and spiders need be mentioned here. In the fish, unusual swimming postures were observed, and in the spiders, alterations in web building were apparently produced by LSD. At very low optimum doses the webs were even better proportioned and more exactly built than normally: however, with higher doses, the webs were badly and rudimentarily made.

How Toxic Is LSD?

The toxicity of LSD has been determined in various animal species. A standard for the toxicity of a substance is the LD_{50}, or the median lethal dose, that is, the dose with which 50 percent of the treated animals die. In general it fluctuates broadly, according to the animal species, and so it is with LSD. The LD_{50} for the mouse amounts to 50–60 mg/kg i.v. (that is, 50 to 60 thousandths of a gram of LSD per kilogram of animal weight upon injection of an LSD solution into the veins). In the rat the LD_{50} drops to 16.5 mg/kg, and in rabbits to 0.3 mg/kg. One elephant given 0.297 g of LSD died after a few minutes. The weight of this animal was determined to be 5,000 kg, which corresponds to a lethal dose of 0.06 mg/kg (0.06 thousandths of a gram per kilogram of body weight). Because this involves only a single case, this value cannot be generalized, but we can at least deduce from it that the largest land animal reacts proportionally very sensitively to LSD, since the lethal dose in elephants must be some 1,000 times lower than in the mouse. Most animals die from a lethal dose of LSD by respiratory arrest.

The minute doses that cause death in animal experiments may give the impression that LSD is a very toxic substance. However, if one compares the lethal dose in animals with the effective dose in human beings, which is 0.0003–0.001 mg/kg (0.0003 to 0.001 thousandths of a gram per kilogram of body weight), this shows an extraordinarily low toxicity for LSD. Only a 300- to 600-fold overdose of LSD, compared to the lethal dose in rabbits, or fully a 50,000- to 100,000-fold overdose, in comparison to the toxicity in the mouse, would have fatal results in human beings. These comparisons of relative toxicity are, to be sure, only understandable as estimates of orders of magnitude, for the determination of the therapeutic index (that is, the ratio between the effective and the lethal dose) is only meaningful within a given species. Such a procedure is not possible in this case because the lethal dose of LSD for humans is not known. To my knowledge, there have not as yet occurred any casualties that are a direct consequence of LSD poisoning. Numerous episodes of fatal consequences attributed to LSD ingestion have indeed been recorded, but these were accidents, even suicides, that may be attributed to the mentally disoriented condition of LSD intoxication. The danger of LSD lies not in its toxicity, but rather in the unpredictability of its psychic effects.

Some years ago reports appeared in the scientific literature and also in the lay press, alleging that damage to chromosomes or the genetic material had been caused by LSD. These effects, however, have been observed in only a few individual cases. Subsequent comprehensive investigations of a large, statistically significant number of cases, however, showed that there was no connection between chromosome anomalies and LSD medication. The same applies to reports about fetal deformities that had allegedly been produced by LSD. In animal experiments, it is indeed possible to induce fetal deformities through extremely high doses of LSD, which lie well above the doses used in human beings. But under these conditions, even harmless substances produce such damage. Examination of reported individual cases of human fetal deformities reveals, again, no connection between LSD use and such injury. If there had been any such connection, it would long since have attracted attention, for several million people by now have taken LSD.

Pharmacological Properties of LSD

LSD is absorbed easily and completely through the gastrointestinal tract. It is therefore unnecessary to inject LSD, except for special purposes. Experiments on mice with radioactively labeled LSD have established that intravenously injected LSD disappeared, down to a small vestige, very rapidly from the bloodstream and was distributed throughout the organism. Unexpectedly, the lowest concentration is found in the brain. It is concentrated here in certain centers of the midbrain that play a role in the regulation of emotion. Such findings give indications as to the localization of certain psychic functions in the brain.

The concentration of LSD in the various organs attains maximum values 10 to 15 minutes after injection, then falls off again swiftly. The small intestine, in which the concentration attains the maximum within two hours, constitutes an exception. The elimination of LSD is conducted for the most part (up to some 80 percent) through the intestine via liver and bile. Only 1 to 10 percent of the elimination product exists as unaltered LSD; the remainder is made up of various transformation products.

As the psychic effects of LSD persist even after it can no longer be detected in the organism, we must assume that LSD is not active as such, but that it rather triggers certain biochemical, neurophysiological, and psychic mechanisms that provoke the inebriated condition and continue in the absence of the active principle.

LSD stimulates centers of the sympathetic nervous system in the midbrain, which leads to pupillary dilatation, increase in body temperature, and rise in the blood-sugar level. The uterine-constricting activity of LSD has already been mentioned.

An especially interesting pharmacological property of LSD, discovered by J. H. Gaddum in England, is its serotonin-blocking effect. Serotonin is a hormone-like substance, occurring naturally in various organs of warm-blooded animals. Concentrated in the midbrain, it plays an important role in the propagation of impulses in certain nerves and therefore in the biochemistry of psychic functions. The disruption of natural functioning of serotonin by LSD was for some time regarded as an explanation of its psychic effects. However, it was soon shown that even certain derivatives of LSD (compounds in which the chemical structure of LSD is slightly modified) that exhibit no hallucinogenic properties, inhibit the effects of serotonin just as strongly, or yet more strongly, than unaltered LSD. The serotonin-blocking effect of LSD thus does not suffice to explain its hallucinogenic properties.

LSD also influences neurophysiological functions that are connected with dopamine, which is, like serotonin, a naturally occurring hormone-like substance. Most of the brain centers receptive to dopamine become activated by LSD, while the others are depressed.

As yet we do not know the biochemical mechanisms

through which LSD exerts its psychic effects. Investigations of the interactions of LSD with brain factors like serotonin and dopamine, however, are examples of how LSD can serve as a tool in brain research, in the study of the biochemical processes that underlie the psychic functions.

3

Chemical Modifications of LSD

When a new type of active compound is discovered in pharmaceutical-chemical research, whether by isolation from a plant drug or from animal organs, or through synthetic production as in the case of LSD, then the chemist attempts, through alterations in its molecular structure, to produce new compounds with similar, perhaps improved activity, or with other valuable active properties. We call this process a *chemical modification* of this type of active substance. Of the approximately 20,000 new substances that are produced annually in the pharmaceutical-chemical research laboratories of the world, the overwhelming majority are modification products of proportionally few types of active compounds. The discovery of a really new type of active substance—new with regard to chemical structure and pharmacological effect—is a rare stroke of luck.

Soon after the discovery of the psychic effects of LSD, two coworkers were assigned to join me in carrying out the chemical modification of LSD on a broader basis and in further investigations in the field of ergot alkaloids. The work on the chemical structure of ergot alkaloids of the peptide type, to which ergotamine and the alkaloids of the ergotoxine group belong, continued with Dr. Theodor Petrzilka. Working with Dr. Franz Troxler, I produced a great number of chemical modifications of LSD, and we attempted to gain further insights into the structure of lysergic acid, for which the American researchers had already proposed a structural formula. In 1949 we succeeded in correcting this formula and specifying the valid structure of this common nucleus of all ergot alkaloids, including of course LSD.

The investigations of the peptide alkaloids of ergot led to the complete structural formulas of these substances, which we published in 1951. Their correctness was confirmed through the total synthesis of ergotamine, which was realized ten years later in collaboration with two younger coworkers, Dr. Albert J. Frey and Dr. Hans Ott. Another coworker, Dr. Paul A. Stadler, was largely responsible for the development of this synthesis into a process practicable on an industrial scale. The synthetic production of peptide ergot alkaloids using lysergic acid obtained from special cultures of the ergot fungus in tanks has great economic importance. This procedure is used to produce the starting material for the medicaments Hydergine and Dihydergot.

Now we return to the chemical modifications of LSD. Many LSD derivatives were produced, since 1945, in collaboration with Dr. Troxler, but none proved hallucinogenically more active than LSD. Indeed, the very closest relatives proved themselves essentially less active in this respect.

There are four different possibilities of spatial arrangement of atoms in the LSD molecule. They are differentiated in technical language by the prefix *iso*- and the letters *D* and *L*. Besides LSD, which is more precisely designated as D-lysergic acid diethylamide, I have also produced and likewise tested in self-experiments the three other spatially different forms, namely D-isolysergic acid diethylamide (iso-LSD), L-lysergic acid diethylamide (L-LSD), and L-isolysergic acid diethylamide (L-iso-LSD). The last three forms of LSD showed no psychic effects up to a dose of 0.5 mg, which corresponds to a 20-fold quantity of a still distinctly active LSD dose.

A substance very closely related to LSD, the monoethylamide of lysergic acid (LAE-23), in which an ethyl group is replaced by a hydrogen atom on the diethylamide residue of LSD, proved to be some ten times less psychoactive than LSD. The hallucinogenic effect of this substance is also qualitatively different: it is characterized by a narcotic component. This narcotic effect is yet more pronounced in lysergic acid amide (LA-111), in which both ethyl groups of LSD are displaced by hydrogen atoms. These effects, which I established in comparative self-experiments with LA-111 and LAE-32, were corroborated by subsequent clinical investigations.

Fifteen years later we encountered lysergic acid amide, which had been produced synthetically for these investigations, as a naturally occurring active principle of the Mexican magic drug *ololiuhqui*. In a later chapter I shall deal more fully with this unexpected discovery.

Certain results of the chemical modification of LSD proved valuable to medicinal research; LSD derivatives were found that were only weakly or not at all hallucinogenic, but instead exhibited other effects of LSD to an increased extent. Such an effect of LSD is its blocking effect on the neurotransmitter serotonin (referred to previously in the discussion of the pharmacological properties of LSD). As serotonin plays a role in allergic-inflammatory processes and also in the generation of migraine, a specific serotonin-blocking substance was of great significance to medicinal research. We therefore searched systematically for LSD derivatives without hallucinogenic effects, but with the highest possible activity as serotonin blockers. The first such active substance was found in bromo-LSD, which has become known in medicinal-biological research under the designation BOL-148. In the course of our investigations on serotonin antagonists, Dr. Troxler produced in the sequel yet stronger and more specifically active compounds. The most active entered the medicinal market as a medicament for the treatment of migraine, under the trademark "Deseril" or, in English-speaking countries, "Sansert."

4

Use of LSD in Psychiatry

Soon after LSD was tried on animals, the first systematic investigation of the substance was carried out on human beings, at the psychiatric clinic of the University of Zurich. Werner A. Stoll, M.D. (a son of Professor Arthur Stoll), who led this research, published his results in 1947 in the *Schweizer Archiv für Neurologie und Psychiatrie*, under the title "Lysergsäure-diäthylamid, ein Phantastikum aus der Mutterkorngruppe" [Lysergic acid diethylamide, a phantasticum from the ergot group].

The tests involved healthy research subjects as well as schizophrenic patients. The dosages—substantially lower than in my first self-experiment with 0.25 mg LSD tartrate—amounted to only 0.02 to 0.13 mg. The emotional state during the LSD inebriation was here predominantly euphoric, whereas in my experiment the mood was marked by grave side effects resulting from overdosage and, of course, fear of the uncertain outcome.

This fundamental publication, which gave a scientific description of all the basic features of LSD inebriation, classified the new active principle as a phantasticum. However, the question of *therapeutic application* of LSD remained unanswered. On the other hand, the report emphasized the extraordinarily high activity of LSD, which corresponds to the activity of trace substances occurring in the organism that are considered to be responsible for certain mental disorders. Another subject discussed in this first publication was the possible application of LSD as a research tool in psychiatry, which follows from its tremendous psychic activity.

First Self-Experiment by a Psychiatrist

In his paper, W. A. Stoll also gave a detailed description of his own personal experiment with LSD. Since this was the first self-experiment published by a psychiatrist, and since it describes many characteristic features of LSD inebriation, it is interesting to quote extensively from the report. I warmly thank the author for kind permission to republish this extract.

> At 8 o'clock I took 60 mcg (0.06 milligrams) of LSD. Some 20 minutes later, the first symptoms appeared: heaviness in the limbs, slight atactic (i.e., confused, uncoordinated) symptoms. A subjectively very unpleasant phase of general malaise followed, in parallel with the drop in blood pressure registered by the examiners.
>
> A certain euphoria then set in, though it seemed weaker to me than experiences in an earlier experiment. The ataxia increased, and I went "sailing" around the room with large strides. I felt somewhat better, but was glad to lie down.

Afterward the room was darkened (dark experiment); there followed an unprecedented experience of unimaginable intensity that kept increasing in strength. It was characterized by an unbelievable profusion of optical hallucinations that appeared and vanished with great speed, to make way for countless new images. I saw a profusion of circles, vortices, sparks, showers, crosses, and spirals in constant, racing flux.

The images appeared to stream in on me predominantly from the center of the visual field, or out of the lower left edge. When a picture appeared in the middle, the remaining field of vision was simultaneously filled up with a vast number of similar visions. All were colored: bright, luminous red, yellow, and green predominated.

I never managed to linger on any picture. When the supervisor of the experiment emphasized my great fantasies, the richness of my statements, I could only react with a sympathetic smile. I knew, in fact, that I could not retain, much less describe, more than a fraction of the pictures. I had to force myself to give a description. Terms such as "fireworks" or "kaleidoscopic" were poor and inadequate. I felt that I had to immerse myself more and more deeply into this strange and fascinating world, in order to allow the exuberance, the unimaginable wealth, to work on me.

At first, the hallucinations were elementary: rays, bundles of rays, rain, rings, vortices, loops, sprays, clouds, etc. Then more highly organized visions also appeared: arches, rows of arches, a sea of roofs, desert landscapes, terraces, flickering fire, starry skies of unbelievable splendor. The original, more simple images continued in the midst of these more highly organized hallucinations. I remember the following images in particular:

A succession of towering, Gothic vaults, an endless choir, of which I could not see the lower portions.

A landscape of skyscrapers, reminiscent of pictures of the entrance to New York harbor: house towers staggered behind and beside one another with innumerable rows of windows. Again the foundation was missing.

A system of masts and ropes, which reminded me of a reproduction of a painting seen the previous day (the inside of a circus tent).

An evening sky of an unimaginable pale blue over the dark roofs of a Spanish city. I had a peculiar feeling of anticipation, was full of joy and decidedly ready for adventure. All at once the stars flared up, amassed, and turned to a dense rain of stars and sparks that streamed toward me. City and sky had disappeared.

I was in a garden, saw brilliant red, yellow, and green lights falling through a dark trelliswork, an indescribably joyous experience.

It was significant that all the images consisted of countless repetitions of the same elements: many sparks, many circles, many arches, many windows, many fires, etc. I never saw isolated images, but always duplications of the same image, endlessly repeated.

I felt myself one with all romanticists and dreamers, thought of E. T. A. Hoffmann, saw the maelstrom of Poe (even though, at the time I had read Poe, his description seemed exaggerated). Often I seemed to stand at the pinnacle of artistic experience; I luxuriated in the colors of the altar of Isenheim, and knew the euphoria and exultation of an artistic vision. I must also have spoken again and again of modern art; I thought of abstract pictures, which all at once I seemed to understand. Then again, there were impressions of an extreme trashiness, both in their shapes and their color combinations. The most garish, cheap modern lamp ornaments and sofa pillows came into my mind. The train of thought was quickened. But I had the feeling the supervisor of the experiment could still keep up with me. Of course I knew, intellectually, that I was rushing him. At first I had descriptions rapidly at hand. With the increasingly frenzied pace, it became impossible to think a thought through to the end. I must have only started many sentences. . . .

When I tried to restrict myself to specific subjects, the experiment proved most unsuccessful. My mind would even focus, in a certain sense, on contrary images: skyscrapers instead of a church, a broad desert instead of a mountain.

I assumed that I had accurately estimated the elapsed time, but did not take the matter very seriously. Such questions did not interest me in the slightest.

My state of mind was consciously euphoric. I enjoyed the condition, was serene, and took a most active interest in the experience. From time to time I opened my eyes. The weak red light seemed mysterious, much more than before. The busily writing research supervisor appeared to me to be very far away. Often I had peculiar bodily sensations: I believed my hands to be attached to some distant body, but was not certain whether it was my own.

After termination of the first dark experiment, I strolled about in the room a bit, was unsure on my legs, and again felt less well. I became cold and was thankful that the research supervisor covered me with a blanket. I felt unkempt, unshaven, and unwashed. The room seemed strange and broad. Later I squatted on a high stool, thinking all the while that I sat there like a bird on the roost.

The supervisor emphasized my own wretched appearance. He seemed remarkably graceful. I myself had small, finely formed hands. As I washed them, it was happening a long way from me, somewhere down below on the right. It was questionable, but utterly unimportant, whether they were my own hands.

In the landscape outside, well known to me, many things appeared to have changed. Besides the hallucinations, I could now see the real as well. Later this was no longer possible, although I remained aware that reality was otherwise. . . .

A barracks, and the garage standing before it to the left, suddenly changed to a landscape of ruins, shattered to pieces. I saw wall wreckage and projecting beams, inspired undoubtedly by the memory of the war events in this region.

In a uniform, extensive field, I kept seeing figures, which I tried to draw, but could get no farther than the crudest beginnings. I saw an extremely opulent sculptural ornamentation in constant metamorphosis, in continuous flux. I was reminded of every possible foreign culture, saw Mexican, Indian motifs. Between a grating of small beams and tendrils appeared little caricatures, idols, masks, strangely mixed all of a sudden with childish drawings of people. The tempo was slackened compared to the dark experiment.

The euphoria had now vanished. I became depressed, especially during the second dark experiment, which followed. Whereas during the first dark experiment, the hallucinations had alternated with great rapidity in bright and luminous colors, now blue, violet, and dark green prevailed. The movement of larger images was slower milder, quieter, although even these were composed of finely raining "elemental dots," which streamed and whirled about quickly. During the first dark experiment, the commotion had frequently intruded upon me; now it often led distinctly away from me into the center of the picture, where a sucking mouth appeared. I saw grottoes with fantastic erosions and stalactites, reminding me of the child's book *Im Wunderreiche des Bergkönigs* [In the wondrous realm of the mountain king]. Serene systems of arches rose up. On the right-hand side, a row of shed roofs suddenly appeared; I thought of an evening ride homeward during military service. Significantly it involved a homeward ride: there was no longer anything like departure or love of adventure. I felt protected, enveloped by motherliness, was in peace. The hallucinations were no longer exciting, but instead mild and attenuated. Somewhat later I had the feeling of possessing the same motherly strength. I perceived an inclination, a desire to help, and behaved then in an exaggeratedly sentimental and trashy manner, where medical ethics are concerned. I realized this and was able to stop.

But the depressed state of mind remained. I tried again and again to see bright and joyful images. But to no avail; only dark blue and green patterns emerged. I longed to imagine bright fire as in the first dark experiment. And I did see fires; however, they were sacrificial fires on the gloomy battlement of a citadel on a remote, autumnal heath. Once I managed to behold a bright ascending multitude of sparks, but at half-altitude it transformed itself into a group of silently moving spots from a peacock's tail. During the experiment I was very impressed that my state of mind and the type of hallucinations harmonized so consistently and uninterruptedly.

During the second dark experiment I observed that random noises, and also noises intentionally produced by the supervisor of the experiment, provoked simultaneous changes in the optical impressions (synesthesia). In the same manner, pressure on the eyeball produced alterations of visual perceptions.

Toward the end of the second dark experiment, I began to watch for sexual fantasies, which were, however, totally absent. In no way could I experience sexual desire. I wanted to imagine a picture of a woman; only a crude modern-primitive sculpture appeared. It seemed completely unerotic, and its forms were immediately replaced by agitated circles and loops.

After the second dark experiment I felt benumbed and physically unwell. I perspired, was exhausted. I was thankful not to have to go to the cafeteria for lunch. The laboratory assistant who brought us the food appeared to me small and distant, of the same remarkable daintiness as the supervisor of the experiment.

Sometime around 3:00 P.M. I felt better, so that the supervisor could pursue his work. With some effort I managed to take notes myself. I sat at the table, wanted to read, but could not concentrate. Once I seemed to myself like a shape from a surrealistic picture, whose limbs were not connected with the body, but were rather painted somewhere close by. . . .

I was depressed and thought with interest of the possibility of suicide. With some terror I apprehended that such thoughts were remarkably familiar to me. It seemed singularly self-evident that a depressed person commits suicide. . . .

On the way home and in the evening I was again euphoric, brimming with the experiences of the morning. I had experienced unexpected, impressive things. It seemed to me that a great epoch of my life had been crowded into a few hours. I was tempted to repeat the experiment.

The next day I was careless in my thinking and conduct, had great trouble concentrating, was apathetic. . . . The casual, slightly dream-like condition persisted into the afternoon. I had great trouble reporting in any organized way on a simple problem. I felt a growing general weariness, an increasing awareness that I had now returned to everyday reality.

The second day after the experiment brought an irresolute state. . . . Mild, but distinct depression was experienced during the following week, a feeling which of course could be related only indirectly to LSD.

The Psychic Effects of LSD

The picture of the activity of LSD obtained from these first investigations was not new to science. It largely matched the commonly held view of mescaline, an alkaloid that had been investigated as early as the turn of the century. Mescaline is the psychoactive constituent of a Mexican cactus *Lophophora williamsii* (syn. *Anhalonium lewinii*). This cactus has been eaten by American Indians ever since pre-Columbian times, and is still used today as a sacred drug in religious ceremonies. In his monograph *Phantastica* (Verlag Georg Stilke, Berlin, 1924), L. Lewin has amply described the history of this drug, called *péyotl* by the Aztecs. The alkaloid mescaline was isolated from the cactus by A. Heffter in 1896, and in 1919 its chemical structure was elucidated and it was produced synthetically by E. Späth. It was the first hallucinogen or phantasticum (as this type of active compound was described by Lewin) to become available as a pure substance, permitting the study of chemically induced changes of sensory perceptions, mental illusions (hallucinations), and alterations of consciousness. In the 1920s extended experiments with mescaline were carried out on animal and human subjects and described comprehensively by K. Beringer in his book *Der Mes-*

44

kalinrausch (Verlag Julius Springer, Berlin, 1927). Because these investigations failed to indicate any applications of mescaline in medicine, interest in this active substance waned.

With the discovery of LSD, hallucinogen research received a new impetus. The novelty of LSD as opposed to mescaline was its high activity, lying in a different order of magnitude. The active dose of mescaline, 0.2 to 0.5 g, is comparable to 0.00002 to 0.0001 g of LSD; in other words, LSD is some 5,000 to 10,000 times more active than mescaline.

LSD's unique position among the psychopharmaceuticals is not only due to its high activity, in a quantitative sense. The substance also has qualitative significance: it manifests a high specificity, that is, an activity aimed specifically at the human psyche. It can be assumed, therefore, that LSD affects the highest control centers of the psychic and intellectual functions.

The psychic effects of LSD, which are produced by such minimal quantities of material, are too meaningful and too multiform to be explained by toxic alterations of brain function. If LSD acted only through a toxic effect on the brain, then LSD experiences would be entirely psychopathological in meaning, without any psychological or psychiatric interest. On the contrary, it is likely that alterations of nerve conductivity and influence on the activity of nerve connections (synapses), which have been experimentally demonstrated, play an important role. This could mean that an influence is being exerted on the extremely complex system of cross-connections and synapses between the many billions of brain cells, the system on which the higher psychic and intellectual functions depend. This would be a promising area to explore in the search for an explanation of LSD's radical efficacy.

The nature of LSD's activity could lead to numerous possibilities of medicinal-psychiatric uses, as W. A. Stoll's ground-breaking studies had already shown. Sandoz therefore made the new active substance available to research institutes and physicians as an experimental drug, giving it the trade name Delysid (*D-Lys*ergsäure-diäthylam*id*) which I had proposed. The printed prospectus below describes possible applications of this kind and voices the necessary precautions.

Delysid (LSD 25)

D-lysergic acid diethylamide tartrate

Sugar-coated tablets containing 0.025 mg. (25 µg.)
Ampoules of 1 ml. containing 0.1 mg. (100 µg.) for oral administration
The solution may also be injected s.c. or i.v. The effect is identical with that of oral administration but sets in more rapidly.

PROPERTIES

The administration of very small doses of Delysid (½-2 µg./kg. body weight) results in transitory disturbances of affect, hallucinations, depersonalization, reliving of repressed memories, and mild neurovegetative symptoms. The effect sets in after 30 to 90 minutes and generally lasts 5 to 12 hours. However, intermittent disturbances of affect may occasionally persist for several days.

METHOD OF ADMINISTRATION

For oral administration the contents of 1 ampoule of Delysid are diluted with distilled water, a 1% solution of tartaric acid or halogen-free tap water. The absorption of the solution is somewhat more rapid and more constant than that of the tablets.

Ampoules which have not been opened, which have been protected against light and stored in a cool place are stable for an unlimited period. Ampoules which have been opened or diluted solutions retain their effectiveness for 1 to 2 days, if stored in a refrigerator.

INDICATIONS AND DOSAGE

a) Analytical psychotherapy, to elicit release of repressed material and provide mental relaxation, particularly in anxiety states and obsessional neuroses.

The initial dose is 25 μg. (¼ of an ampoule or 1 tablet). This dose is increased at each treatment by 25 μg. until the optimum dose (usually between 50 and 200 μg.) is found. The individual treatments are best given at intervals of one week.

b) Experimental studies on the nature of psychoses: By taking Delysid himself, the psychiatrist is able to gain an insight into the world of ideas and sensations of mental patients. Delysid can also be used to induce model psychoses of short duration in normal subjects, thus facilitating studies on the pathogenesis of mental disease.

In normal subjects, doses of 25 to 75 μg. are generally sufficient to produce a hallucinatory psychosis (on an average 1 μg./kg. body weight). In certain forms of psychosis and in chronic alcoholism, higher doses are necessary (2 to 4 μg./ kg. body weight).

PRECAUTIONS

Pathological mental conditions may be intensified by Delysid. Particular caution is necessary in subjects with a suicidal tendency and in those cases where a psychotic development appears imminent.

The psycho-affective liability and the tendency to commit impulsive acts may occasionally last for some days.

Delysid should only be administered under strict medical supervision. The supervision should not be discontinued until the effects of the drug have completely worn off.

ANTIDOTE

The mental effects of Delysid can be rapidly reversed by the i.m. administration of 50 mg. chlorpromazine.

Literature available on request.

SANDOZ LTD., BASLE, SWITZERLAND

The use of LSD in analytical psychotherapy is based mainly on the following psychic effects.

In LSD inebriation the accustomed world view undergoes a deep-seated transformation and disintegration. Connected with this is a loosening or even suspension of the I-you barrier. Patients who are bogged down in an egocentric problem cycle can thereby be helped to release themselves from their fixation and isolation. The result can be an improved rapport with the doctor and a greater susceptibility to psychotherapeutic influence. The enhanced suggestibility under the influence of LSD works toward the same goal.

Another significant, psychotherapeutically valuable characteristic of LSD inebriation is the tendency of long forgotten or suppressed contents of experience to appear again in consciousness. Traumatic events, which are sought in psychoanalysis, may then become accessible to psychotherapeutic treatment. Numerous case histories tell of experiences from even the earliest childhood that were vividly recalled during psychoanalysis under the influence of LSD. This does not involve an ordinary recollection, but rather a true reliving; not a *réminiscence*, but rather a *réviviscence*, as the French psychiatrist Jean Delay has formulated it.

LSD does not act as a true medicament; rather it plays the role of a drug aid in the context of psychoanalytic and psychotherapeutic treatment and serves to channel the treatment more effectively and to shorten its duration. It can fulfill this function in two particular ways.

In one procedure, which was developed in European clinics and given the name *psycholytic therapy*, moderately strong doses of LSD are administered in several successive sessions at regular intervals. Subsequently the LSD experiences are worked out in group discussions, and in expression therapy by drawing and painting. The term *psycholytic therapy* was coined by Ronald A. Sandison, an English therapist of Jungian orientation and a pioneer of clinical LSD research. The root *-lysis* or *-lytic* signifies the dissolution of tension or conflicts in the human psyche.

In a second procedure, which is the favored treatment in the United States, a single, very high LSD dose (0.3 to 0.6 mg) is administered after correspondingly intensive psychological preparation of the patients. This method, described as *psychedelic therapy*, attempts to induce a mystical-religious experience through the shock effects of LSD. This experience can then serve as a starting point for a restructuring and curing of the patient's personality in the accompanying psychotherapeutic treatment. The term *psychedelic*, which can be translated as "mind-manifesting" or "mind-expanding," was introduced by Humphry Osmond, a pioneer of LSD research in the United States.

LSD's apparent benefits as a drug auxiliary in psychoanalysis and psychotherapy are derived from properties diametrically opposed to the effects of tranquilizer-type psychopharmaceuticals. Whereas tranquilizers tend to cover up the patient's problems and conflicts, reducing their apparent gravity and importance: LSD, on the contrary, makes them more exposed and more intensely experienced. This clearer recognition of problems and conflicts makes them, in turn, more susceptible to psychotherapeutic treatment.

The suitability and success of LSD in psychoanalysis and psychotherapy are still a subject of controversy in professional circles. The same could be said, however, of other procedures employed in psychiatry such as electroshock, insulin therapy, or psychosurgery, procedures that entail, moreover, a far greater risk than the use of LSD, which under suitable conditions can be considered practically safe.

Because forgotten or repressed experiences, under the influence of LSD, may become conscious with considerable speed, the treatment can be correspondingly shortened. To some psychiatrists, however, this reduction of the therapy's duration is a disadvantage. They are of the opinion that this precipitation leaves the patient insufficient time for psychotherapeutic working-through. The therapeutic effect they believe, persists for a shorter time than when there is a gradual treatment, including a slow process of becoming conscious of the traumatic experiences.

Psycholytic and especially psychedelic therapy require thorough preparation of the patient for the LSD experience, to avoid his or her being frightened by the unusual and the unfamiliar. Only then is a positive interpretation of the experience possible. The selection of patients is also important, since not all types of psychic disturbance respond equally well to these methods of treatment. Successful use of LSD-assisted psychoanalysis and psychotherapy presupposes specific knowledge and experience.

In this respect self-examination by psychiatrists, as W. A. Stoll has pointed out, can be most useful. They provide the doctors with direct insight, based on firsthand experience into the strange world of LSD inebriation, and make it possible for them truly to understand these phenomena in their patients, to interpret them properly, and to take full advantage of them.

The following pioneers in use of LSD as a drug aid in psychoanalysis and psychotherapy deserve to be named in the front rank: A. K. Busch and W. C. Johnson, S. Cohen and B. Eisner, H. A. Abramson, H. Osmond, and A. Hoffer in the United States; R. A. Sandison in England; W. Frederking and H. Leuner in Germany; and G. Roubicek and S. Grof in Czechoslovakia.

The second indication for LSD cited in the Sandoz prospectus on Delysid concerns its use in experimental investigations on the nature of psychoses. This arises from the fact that extraordinary psychic states experimentally produced by LSD in healthy research subjects are similar to many manifestations of certain mental disturbances. In the early days of LSD research, it was often claimed that LSD inebriation has something to do with a type of "model psychosis." This idea was dismissed, however, because extended comparative investigations showed that there were essential differences between the manifestations of psychosis and the LSD experience. With the LSD model, nevertheless, it is possible to study deviations from the normal psychic and mental condition, and to observe the biochemical and electrophysiological alterations associated with them. Perhaps we shall thereby gain new insights into the nature of psychoses. According to certain theories, various mental disturbances could be produced by psychotoxic metabolic products that have the power, even in minimal quantities, to alter the functions of brain cells. LSD represents a substance that certainly does not occur in the human organism, but whose existence and activity let it seem possible that abnormal metabolic products could exist, that even in trace quantities could produce mental disturbances. As a result, the conception of a biochemical origin of certain mental disturbances has received broader support, and research in this direction has been stimulated.

One medicinal use of LSD that touches on fundamental ethical questions is its administration to the dying. This practice arose from observations in American clinics that especially severe painful conditions of cancer patients, which no longer respond to conventional pain-relieving medication, could be alleviated or completely abolished by LSD. Of course, this does not involve an analgesic effect in the true sense. The diminution of pain sensitivity may rather occur because patients under the influence of LSD are psychologically so dissociated from their bodies that physical pain no longer penetrates their consciousness. In order for LSD to be effective in such cases, it is especially crucial that patients be prepared and instructed about the kind of experiences and transformations that await them. In many cases it has proved beneficial for either a member of the clergy or a psychotherapist to guide the patient's thoughts in a religious direction. Numerous case histories tell of patients who gained meaningful insights about life and death on their deathbeds as, freed from pain in

LSD ecstasy and reconciled to their fate, they faced their earthly demise fearlessly and in peace.

The hitherto existing knowledge about the administration of LSD to the terminally ill has been summarized and published by S. Grof and J. Halifax in their book *The Human Encounter with Death* (E. P. Dutton, New York, 1977). The authors, together with E. Kast, S. Cohen, and W. A. Pahnke, are among the pioneers of this application of LSD.

The most recent comprehensive publication on the use of LSD in psychiatry, *Realms of the Human Unconscious: Observations from LSD Research* (The Viking Press, New York, 1975), likewise comes from S. Grof, the Czech psychiatrist who has emigrated to the United States. This book offers a critical evaluation of the LSD experience from the viewpoint of Freud and Jung, as well as of existential analysis.

5

From Remedy to Inebriant

During the first years after its discovery, LSD brought me the same happiness and gratification that any pharmaceutical chemist would feel on learning that a substance he or she produced might possibly develop into a valuable medicament. For the creation of new remedies is the goal of a pharmaceutical chemist's research activity; therein lies the meaning of his or her work.

Nonmedical Use of LSD

This joy at having fathered LSD was tarnished after more than ten years of uninterrupted scientific research and medicinal use when LSD was swept up in the huge wave of an inebriant mania that began to spread over the Western world, above all the United States, at the end of the 1950s. It was strange how rapidly LSD adopted its new role as inebriant and, for a time, became the number-one inebriating drug, at least as far as publicity was concerned. The more its use as an inebriant was disseminated, bringing an upsurge in the number of untoward incidents caused by careless, medically unsupervised use, the more LSD became a problem child for me and for the Sandoz firm.

It was obvious that a substance with such fantastic effects on mental perception and on the experience of the outer and inner world would also arouse interest outside medical science, but I had not expected that LSD, with its unfathomably uncanny, profound effects, so unlike the character of a recreational drug, would ever find worldwide use as an inebriant. I had expected curiosity and interest on the part of artists outside of medicine—performers, painters, and writers—but not among people in general. After the scientific publications around the turn of the century on mescaline—which, as already mentioned, evokes psychic effects quite like those of LSD—the use of this compound remained confined to medicine and to experiments within artistic and literary circles. I had expected the same fate for LSD. And indeed, the first non-medicinal self-experiments with LSD were carried out by writers, painters, musicians, and other intellectuals.

LSD sessions had reportedly provoked extraordinary aesthetic experiences and granted new insights into the essence of the creative process. Artists were influenced in their creative work in unconventional ways. A particular type of art developed that has become known as psychedelic art. It comprises creations produced under the influenced of LSD and other psychedelic drugs, whereby the drugs acted as stimulus and source of inspiration. The standard publication in this field is the book by Robert E. L. Masters and Jean Houston, *Psychedelic Art* (Balance House, 1968). Works of psychedelic art are not created while the drug is in effect, but only afterward, the artist being inspired by these experiences. As long as the inebriated condition lasts, creative activity is impeded, if not completely halted. The influx of images is too great and is increasing too rapidly to be portrayed and fashioned. An overwhelming vision paralyzes activity. Artistic productions arising directly from LSD inebriation, therefore, are mostly rudimentary in character and deserve consideration not because of their artistic merit, but because they are a type of psychoprogram, which offers insight into the deepest mental structures of the artist, activated and made conscious by LSD. This was demonstrated later in a large-scale experiment by the Munich psychiatrist Richard P. Hartmann, in which thirty famous painters took part. He published the results in his book *Malerei aus Bereichen des Unbewussten: Künstler Experimentieren unter LSD* [Painting from spheres of the unconscious: artists experiment with LSD], Verlag M. Du Mont Schauberg, Cologne, 1974).

LSD experiments also gave new impetus to exploration into the essence of religious and mystical experience. Religious scholars and philosophers discussed the question whether the religious and mystical experiences often discovered in LSD sessions were genuine, that is, comparable to spontaneous mysticoreligious enlightenment.

This nonmedicinal yet earnest phase of LSD research, at times in parallel with medicinal research, at times following it, was increasingly overshadowed at the beginning of the 1960s, as LSD use spread with epidemic-like speed through all social classes, as a sensational inebriating drug, in the course of the inebriant mania in the United States. The rapid rise of drug use, which had its beginning in this country about twenty years ago, was not, however, a consequence of the discovery of LSD, as superficial observers often declared. Rather it had deep-seated sociological causes: materialism, alienation from nature through industrialization and increasing urbanization, lack of satisfaction in professional employment in a mechanized, lifeless working world, ennui and purposelessness in a wealthy, saturated society, and lack of a religious, nurturing, and meaningful philosophical foundation of life.

The existence of LSD was even regarded by the drug enthusiasts as a predestined coincidence—it had to be discovered precisely at this time in order to bring help to people suffering under the modern conditions. It is not surprising that LSD first came into circulation as an inebriating drug in the United States, the country in which industrialization, urbanization, and mechanization, even of agriculture, are most broadly advanced. These are the same factors that have led to the origin and growth of the hippie movement that developed simultaneously with the LSD wave. The two cannot be dissociated. It would be worth investigating to what extent the consumption of psychedelic drugs furthered the hippie movement and conversely.

The spread of LSD from medicine and psychiatry into the drug scene was introduced and expedited by publications on sensational LSD experiments that, although they were carried out in psychiatric clinics and universities, were not then reported in scientific journals, but rather in magazines and daily papers, greatly elaborated. Reporters made themselves available as guinea pigs. Sidney Katz, for example, participated in an LSD experiment in the Saskatchewan Hospital in Canada under the supervision of noted psychiatrists; his experiences, however, were not published in a medical journal. Instead, he described them in an article entitled "My Twelve Hours as a Madman" in his magazine *MacLean's Canada National Magazine*, colorfully illustrated in fanciful fullness of detail. The widely distributed German magazine *Quick*, in its issue number 12 of 21 March 1954, reported a sensational eyewitness account on "Ein kühnes wissenschaftliches Experiment" [a daring scientific experiment] by the painter Wilfried Zeller, who took "a few drops of lysergic acid" in the Viennese University Psychiatric Clinic. Of the numerous publications of this type that have made effective lay propaganda for LSD, it is sufficient to cite just one more example: a large-scale, illustrated article in *Look* magazine of September 1959. Entitled "The Curious Story Behind the New Cary Grant," it must have contributed enormously to the diffusion of LSD consumption. The famous movie star had received LSD in a respected clinic in California, in the course of a psychotherapeutic treatment. He informed the *Look* reporter that he had sought inner peace his whole life long, but yoga, hypnosis, and mysticism had not helped him. Only the treatment with LSD had made a new, self-strengthened man out of him, so that after three frustrating marriages he now believed himself really able to love and make a woman happy.

The evolution of LSD from remedy to inebriating drug was, however, primarily promoted by the activities of Dr. Timothy Leary and Dr. Richard Alpert of Harvard University. In a later section I will come to speak in more detail about Dr. Leary and my meetings with this personage who has become known worldwide as an apostle of LSD.

Books also appeared on the U.S. market in which the fantastic effects of LSD were reported more fully. Here only two of the most important will be mentioned: *Exploring Inner Space* by Jane Dunlap (Harcourt Brace and World, New York, 1961) and *My Self and I* by

Constance A. Newland (N.A.L. Signet Books, New York, 1963). Although in both cases LSD was used within the scope of a psychiatric treatment, the authors addressed their books, which became best-sellers, to the broad public. In her book, subtitled "The Intimate and Completely Frank Record of One Woman's Courageous Experiment with Psychiatry's Newest Drug, LSD 25," Constance A. Newland described in intimate detail how she had been cured of frigidity. After such avowals, one can easily imagine that many people would want to try the wondrous medicine for themselves. The mistaken opinion created by such reports—that it would be sufficient simply to take LSD in order to accomplish such miraculous effects and transformations in oneself— soon led to broad diffusion of self-experimentation with the new drug.

Objective, informative books about LSD and its problems also appeared, such as the excellent work by the psychiatrist Dr. Sidney Cohen, *The Beyond Within* (Atheneum, New York, 1967), in which the dangers of careless use are clearly exposed. This had, however, no power to put a stop to the LSD epidemic.

As LSD experiments were often carried out in ignorance of the uncanny, unforeseeable, profound effects, and without medical supervision, they frequently came to a bad end. With increasing LSD consumption in the drug scene, there came an increase in "horror trips"—LSD experiments that led to disoriented conditions and panic, often resulting in accidents and even crime.

The rapid rise of nonmedicinal LSD consumption at the beginning of the 1960s was also partly attributable to the fact that the drug laws then current in most countries did not include LSD. For this reason, drug habitués changed from the legally proscribed narcotics to the still-legal substance LSD. Moreover, the last of the Sandoz patents for the production of LSD expired in 1963, removing a further hindrance to illegal manufacture of the drug.

The rise of LSD in the drug scene caused our firm a nonproductive, laborious burden. National control laboratories and health authorities requested statements from us about chemical and pharmacological properties, stability and toxicity of LSD, and analytical methods for its detection in confiscated drug samples, as well as in the human body, in blood and urine. This brought a voluminous correspondence, which expanded in connection with inquiries from all over the world about accidents, poisonings, criminal acts, and so forth, resulting from misuse of LSD. All this meant enormous, unprofitable difficulties, which the business management of Sandoz regarded with disapproval. Thus it happened one day that Professor Stoll, managing director of the firm at the time, said to me reproachfully: "I would rather you had not discovered LSD."

At that time, I was now and again assailed by doubts whether the valuable pharmacological and psychic effects of LSD might be outweighed by its dangers and by possible injuries due to misuse. Would LSD become a blessing for humanity, or a curse? This I often asked myself when I thought about my problem child. My other preparations, Methergine, Dihydroergotamine, and Hydergine, caused me no such problems and difficulties. They were not problem children; lacking extravagant properties leading to misuse, they have developed in a satisfying manner into therapeutically valuable medicines.

The publicity about LSD attained its high point in the years 1964 to 1966, not only with regard to enthusiastic claims about the wondrous effects of LSD by drug fanatics and hippies, but also to reports of accidents, mental breakdowns, criminal acts, murders, and suicide under the influence of LSD. A veritable LSD hysteria reigned.

Sandoz Stops LSD Distribution

In view of this situation, the management of Sandoz was forced to make a public statement on the LSD problem and to publish accounts of the corresponding measures that had been taken. The pertinent letter, dated 23 August 1965, by Dr. A. Cerletti, at the time director of the Pharmaceutical Department of Sandoz, is reproduced below:

Decision Regarding LSD 25 and Other Hallucinogenic Substances

More than twenty years have elapsed since the discovery by Albert Hofmann of LSD 25 in the SANDOZ Laboratories. Whereas the fundamental importance of this discovery may be assessed by its impact on the development of modern psychiatric research, it must be recognized that it placed a heavy burden of responsibility on SANDOZ, the owner of this product.

The finding of a new chemical with outstanding biological properties, apart from the scientific success implied by its synthesis, is usually the first decisive step toward profitable development of a new drug. In the case of LSD, however, it soon became clear that, despite the outstanding properties of this compound, or rather because of the very nature of these qualities, even though LSD was fully protected by SANDOZ-owned patents since the time of its first synthesis in 1938, the usual means of practical exploitation could not be envisaged.

On the other hand, all the evidence obtained following the initial studies in animals and humans carried out in the SANDOZ research laboratories pointed to the important role that this substance could play as an investigational tool in neurological research and in psychiatry.

It was therefore decided to make LSD available free of charge to qualified experimental and clinical investigators all over the world. This broad research approach was assisted by the provision of any necessary technical aid and in many instances also by financial support.

An enormous amount of scientific documents, published mainly in the international biochemical and medical literature and systematically listed in the "SANDOZ Bibliography on LSD" as well as in the "Catalogue of Literature on Delysid" periodically edited by SANDOZ, gives vivid proof of what has been achieved by following this line of policy over nearly two decades. By exercising this kind of "nobile officium" in accordance with the highest standards of medical ethics with all kinds of self-imposed precautions and restrictions, it was possible for many years to avoid the danger of abuse (i.e., use by people neither competent nor qualified), which is always inherent in a compound with exceptional CNS activity.

In spite of all our precautions, cases of LSD abuse have occurred from time to time in varying circumstances completely beyond the control of SANDOZ. Very recently this danger has increased considerably and in some parts of the world has reached the scale of a serious threat to public health. This state of affairs has now reached a critical point for the following reasons: (1) A worldwide spread of misconceptions of LSD has been caused by an increasing amount of publicity aimed at provoking an active interest in laypeople by means of sensational stories and statements; (2) In most countries no adequate legislation exists to control and regulate the production and distribution of substances like LSD; (3) The problem of availability of LSD, once limited on technical grounds, has fundamentally changed with the advent of mass production of lysergic acid by fermentation procedures. Since the last patent on LSD expired in 1963, it is not surprising to find that an increasing number of dealers in fine chemicals are offering LSD from unknown sources at the high price known to be paid by LSD fanatics.

Taking into consideration all the above-mentioned circumstances and the flood of requests for LSD which has now become uncontrollable, the pharmaceutical management of SANDOZ has decided to stop immediately all further production and distribution of LSD. The same policy will apply to all derivatives or analogues of LSD with hallucinogenic properties as well as to Psilocybin, Psilocin, and their hallucinogenic congeners.

For a while the distribution of LSD and psilocybin was stopped completely by Sandoz. Most countries had subsequently proclaimed strict regulations concerning possession, distribution, and use of hallucinogens, so that physicians, psychiatric clinics, and research institutes, if they could produce a special permit to work with these substances from the respective national health authorities, could again be supplied with LSD and psilocybin. In the United States the National Institute of Mental Health (NIMH) undertook the distribution of these agents to licensed research institutes.

All these legislative and official precautions, however, had little influence on LSD consumption in the drug scene, yet on the other hand hindered and continue to hinder medicinal-psychiatric use and LSD research in biology and neurology, because many researchers dread the red tape that is connected with the procurement of a license for the use of LSD. The bad reputation of LSD—its depiction as an "insanity drug" and a "satanic invention"—constitutes a further reason why many doctors shunned use of LSD in their psychiatric practice.

In the course of recent years the uproar of publicity about LSD has quieted, and the consumption of LSD as an inebriant has also diminished, as far as that can be concluded from the rare reports about accidents and other regrettable occurrences following LSD ingestion. It may be that the decrease of LSD accidents, however, is not simply due to a decline in LSD consumption. Possibly the recreational users, with time, have become more aware of the particular effects and dangers of LSD and more cautious in their use of this drug. Certainly LSD, which was for a time considered in the Western world, above all in the United States, to be the number-one inebriant, has relinquished this leading role to other inebriants such as hashish and the habituating, even physically destructive drugs like heroin and amphetamine. The last-mentioned drugs represent an alarming sociological and public health problem today.

Dangers of Nonmedicinal LSD Experiments

While professional use of LSD in psychiatry entails hardly any risk, the ingestion of this substance outside of medical practice, without medical supervision, is subject to multifarious dangers. These dangers reside, on the one hand, in external circumstances connected with illegal drug use and, on the other hand, in the peculiarity of LSD's psychic effects.

The advocates of uncontrolled, free use of LSD and other hallucinogens base their attitude on two claims: (1) this type of drug produces no addiction, and (2) until now no danger to health from moderate use of hallucinogens has been demonstrated. Both are true. Genuine addiction, characterized by the fact that psychic and often severe physical disturbances appear on withdrawal of the drug, has not been observed, even in cases in which LSD was taken often and over a long period of time. No organic injury or death as a direct consequence of an LSD intoxication has yet been reported. As discussed in greater detail in the chapter "LSD in Animal Experiments and Biological Research," LSD is actually a relatively nontoxic substance in proportion to its extraordinarily high psychic activity.

Psychotic Reactions

Like the other hallucinogens, however, LSD is dangerous in an entirely different sense. While the psychic and physical dangers of the addicting narcotics, the opiates, amphetamines, and so forth, appear only with chronic use, the possible danger of LSD exists in every single experiment. This is because severe disoriented states can appear during any LSD inebriation. It is true that through careful preparation of the experiment and the experimenter such episodes can largely be avoided, but they cannot be excluded with certainty. LSD crises resemble psychotic attacks with a manic or depressive character.

In the manic, hyperactive condition, the feeling of omnipotence or invulnerability can lead to serious casualties. Such accidents have occurred when inebriated persons confused in this way—believing themselves to be invulnerable—walked in front of a moving automobile or jumped out a window in the belief that they were able to fly. This type of LSD casualty, however, is not so common as one might be led to think on the basis of reports that were sensationally exaggerated by the mass media. Nevertheless, such reports must serve as serious warnings.

On the other hand, a report that made the rounds worldwide, in 1966, about an alleged murder committed under the influence on LSD, cannot be true. The suspect, a young man in New York accused of having killed his mother-in-law, explained at his arrest, immediately after the fact, that he knew nothing of the crime and that he had been on an LSD trip for three days. But an LSD inebriation, even with the highest doses, lasts no longer than twelve hours, and repeated ingestion leads to tolerance, which means that extra doses are ineffective. Besides, LSD inebriation is characterized by the fact that the person remembers exactly what he or she has experienced. Presumably the defendant in this case expected leniency for extenuating circumstances, owing to unsoundness of mind.

The danger of a psychotic reaction is especially great if LSD is given to someone without his or her knowledge. This was demonstrated in an episode that took place soon after the discovery of LSD, during the first investigations with the new substance in the Zurich University Psychiatric Clinic, when people were not yet aware of the danger of such jokes. A young doctor, whose colleagues had slipped LSD into his coffee as a lark, wanted to swim across Lake Zurich during the winter at −20°C (−4°F) and had to be prevented by force.

There is a different danger when the LSD-induced disorientation exhibits a depressive rather than manic character. In the course of such an LSD experiment, frightening visions, death agony, or the fear of becoming insane can lead to a threatening psychic breakdown or even to suicide. Here the LSD trip becomes a "horror trip."

The demise of a Dr. Olson, who had been given LSD without his knowledge in the course of U.S. Army drug experiments, and who then committed suicide by jumping from a window, caused a particular sensation. His family could not understand how this quiet, well-adjusted man could have been driven to this deed. Not until fifteen years later, when the secret documents about the experiments were published, did they learn the true circumstances, whereupon the president of the United States publicly apologized to the dependents.

The conditions for the positive outcome of an LSD experiment, with little possibility of a psychotic derailment, reside on the one hand in the individual and on the other hand in the external milieu of the experiment. The internal, personal factors are called set, the external conditions setting.

The beauty of a living room or of an outdoor location is perceived with particular force because of the highly stimulated sense organs during LSD inebriation, and such an amenity has a substantial influence on the course of the experiment. The persons present, their appearance, their traits, are also part of the setting that determines the experience. The acoustic milieu is equally significant. Even harmless noises can turn to torment, and conversely lovely music can develop into a euphoric experience. With LSD experiments in ugly or noisy surroundings, however, there is greater danger of a negative outcome, including psychotic crises. The machine- and appliance-world of today offers much scenery and all types of noise that could very well trigger panic during enhanced sensibility.

Just as meaningful as the external milieu of the LSD experience, if not even more important, is the mental condition of the experimenters, their current state of mind, their attitude to the drug experience, and their expectations associated with it. Even unconscious feelings of happiness or fear can have an effect. LSD tends to intensify the actual psychic state. A feeling of happiness can be heightened to bliss, a depression can deepen to despair. LSD is thus the most inappropriate means imaginable for curing a depressive state. It is dangerous to take LSD in a disturbed, unhappy frame of mind, or in a state of fear. The probability that the experiment will end in a psychic breakdown is then quite high.

Among persons with unstable personality structures, tending to psychotic reactions, LSD experimentation ought to be completely avoided. Here an LSD shock, by releasing a latent psychosis, can produce a lasting mental injury.

The psyche of very young persons should also be considered as unstable, in the sense of not yet having matured. In any case, the shock of such a powerful stream of new and strange perceptions and feelings, such as is engendered by LSD, endangers the sensitive, still-developing psycho-organism. Even the medicinal use of LSD in youths under eighteen years of age, in the scope of psychoanalytic or psychotherapeutic treatment, is discouraged in professional circles, correctly so in my opinion. Juveniles for the most part still lack a secure, solid relationship to reality. Such a relationship is needed before the dramatic experience of new dimensions of reality can be meaningfully integrated into the world view. Instead of leading to a broadening and deepening of reality consciousness, such an experience in adolescents will lead to insecurity and a feeling of being lost. Because of the freshness of sensory perception in youth and the still-unlimited capacity for experience, spontaneous visionary experiences occur much more frequently than in later life. For this reason as well, psychostimulating agents should not be used by juveniles.

Even in healthy, adult persons, even with adherence to all of the preparatory and protective measures discussed, an LSD experiment can fail, causing psychotic reactions. Medical supervision is therefore earnestly to be recommended, even for nonmedicinal LSD experiments. This should include an examination of the state of health before the experiment. The doctor need not be present at the session; however, medical help should at all times be readily available.

Acute LSD psychoses can be cut short and brought under control quickly and reliably by injection of chlorpromazine or another sedative of this type.

The presence of a familiar person, who can request medical help in the event of an emergency, is also an indispensable psychological assurance. Although the LSD inebriation is characterized mostly by an immersion in the individual inner world, a deep need for human contact sometimes arises, especially in depressive phases.

LSD from the Black Market

Nonmedicinal LSD consumption can bring dangers of an entirely different type than hitherto discussed: for most of the LSD offered in the drug scene is of unknown origin. LSD preparations from the black market are unreliable when it comes to both quality and dosage. They rarely contain the declared quantity, but mostly have less LSD, often none at all, and sometimes even too much. In many cases other drugs or even poisonous substances are sold as LSD. These observations were made in our laboratory upon analysis of a great number of LSD samples from the black market. They coincide with the experiences of national drug control departments.

The unreliability in the strength of LSD preparations on the illicit drug market can lead to dangerous overdosage. Overdoses have often proved to be the cause of failed LSD experiments that led to severe psychic and physical breakdowns. Reports of alleged fatal LSD poisoning, however, have yet to be confirmed. Close scrutiny of such cases invariably established other causative factors.

The following case, which took place in 1970, is cited as an example of the possible dangers of black market LSD. We received for investigation from the police a drug powder distributed as LSD. It came from a young man who was admitted to the hospital in critical condition and whose friend had also ingested this preparation and died as a result. Analysis showed that the powder contained no LSD, but rather the very poisonous alkaloid strychnine.

If most black market LSD preparations contained less than the stated quantity and often no LSD at all, the reason is either deliberate falsification or the great instability of this substance. LSD is very sensitive to air and light. It is oxidatively destroyed by the oxygen in the air and is transformed into an inactive substance under the influence of light. This must be taken into account during the synthesis and especially during the production of stable, storable forms of LSD. Claims that LSD may easily be prepared, or that every chemistry student in a half-decent laboratory is capable of producing it, are untrue. Procedures for synthesis of LSD have indeed been published and are accessible to everyone. With these detailed procedures in hand, chemists would be able to carry out the synthesis, provided they had pure lysergic acid at their disposal; its possession today, however, is subject to the same strict regulations as LSD. In order to isolate LSD in pure crystalline form from the reaction solution and in order to produce stable preparations, however, special equipment and not easily acquired specific experience are required, owing (as stated previously) to the great instability of this substance.

Only in completely oxygen-free ampules protected from light is LSD absolutely stable. Such ampules, containing 100 μg (= 0.1 mg) LSD-tartrate (tartaric acid salt of LSD) in 1 cc of aqueous solution, were produced for biological research and medicinal use by the Sandoz firm. LSD in tablets prepared with additives that inhibit oxidation, while not absolutely stable, at least keeps for a longer time. But LSD preparations often found on the black market—LSD that has been applied in solution onto sugar cubes or blotting paper—decompose in the course of weeks or a few months.

With such a highly potent substance as LSD, the correct dosage is of paramount importance. Here the tenet of Paracelsus holds good: the dose determines whether a substance acts as a remedy or as a poison. A controlled dosage, however, is not possible with preparations from the black market, whose active strength is in no way guaranteed. One of the greatest dangers of non-medicinal LSD experiments lies, therefore, in the use of such preparations of unknown provenience.

The Case of Dr. Leary

Dr. Timothy Leary, who has become known worldwide in his role of drug apostle, had an extraordinarily strong influence on the diffusion of illegal LSD consumption in the United States. On the occasion of a vacation in Mexico in the year 1960, Leary had eaten the legendary "sacred mushrooms," which he had purchased from a shaman. During the mushroom inebriation he entered into a state of mystico-religious ecstasy, which he described as the deepest religious experience of his life. From then on, Dr. Leary, who at the time was a lecturer in psychology at Harvard University in Cambridge, Massachusetts, dedicated himself totally to research on the effects and possibilities of the use of psychedelic drugs. Together with his colleague Dr. Richard Alpert, he started various research projects at the university, in which LSD and psilocybin, isolated by us in the meantime, were employed.

The reintegration of convicts into society, the production of mystico-religious experiences in theologians and members of the clergy, and the furtherance of creativity in artists and writers with the help of LSD and psilocybin were tested with scientific methodology. Even persons like Aldous Huxley, Arthur Koestler, and Allen Ginsberg participated in these investigations. Particular consideration was given to the question, to what degree mental preparation and expectation of the subjects, along with the external milieu of the experiment, are able to influence the course and character of states of psychedelic inebriation.

In January 1963, Dr. Leary sent me a detailed report of these studies, in which he enthusiastically imparted the positive results obtained and gave expression to his beliefs in the advantages and very promising possibilities of such use of these active compounds. At the same time, the Sandoz firm received an inquiry about the supply of 100g LSD and 25 kg psilocybin, signed by Dr. Timothy Leary, from the Harvard University Department of Social Relations. The requirement for such an enormous quantity (the stated amounts correspond to 1 million doses of LSD and 2.5 million doses of psilocybin) was based on the planned extension of investigations to tissue, organ, and animal studies. We made the supply of these substances contingent upon the production of an import license on behalf of the U.S. health authorities. Immediately we received the order for the stated quantities of LSD and psilocybin, along with a check for $10,000 as deposit but without the required import license. Dr. Leary signed for this order, but no longer as lecturer at Harvard University, rather as president of an organization he had recently founded, the International Federation for Internal Freedom (IFIF). Because, in addition, our inquiry to the appropriate dean of Harvard University had shown that the university authorities did not approve of the continuation of the research project by Leary and Alpert, we canceled our offer upon return of the deposit.

Shortly thereafter, Leary and Alpert were discharged from the teaching staff of Harvard University because the investigations, at first conducted in an academic milieu, had lost their scientific character. The experiments had turned into LSD parties.

The LSD trip—LSD as a ticket to an adventurous journey into new worlds of mental and physical experience—became the latest exciting fashion among academic youth, spreading rapidly from Harvard to other universities. Leary's doctrine—that LSD not only served to find the divine and to discover the self, but indeed was the most potent aphrodisiac yet discovered—surely contributed quite decisively to the rapid propagation of LSD consumption among the younger generation. Later, in an interview with the monthly magazine *Playboy*, Leary said that the intensification of sexual experience and the potentiation of sexual ecstasy by LSD was one of the chief reasons for the LSD boom.

After his expulsion from Harvard University, Leary was completely transformed from a psychology lecturer pursuing research, into the messiah of the psychedelic movement. He and his friends of the IFIF founded a psychedelic research center in lovely, scenic surroundings in Zihuatanejo, Mexico. I received a personal invitation from Dr. Leary to participate in a top-level planning session on psychedelic drugs, scheduled to take place there in August 1963. I would gladly have accepted this grand invitation, in which I was offered reimbursement for travel expenses and free lodging, in order to learn from personal observation the methods, operation, and the entire atmosphere of such a psychedelic research center, about which contradictory, to some extent very remarkable, reports were then circulating. Unfortunately, professional obligations kept me at that moment from flying to Mexico to get a picture at first hand of the controversial enterprise. The Zihuatanejo Research Center did not last long. Leary and his adherents were expelled from the country by the Mexican government. Leary, however, who had now become not only the messiah but also the martyr of the psychedelic movement, soon received help from the young New York millionaire William Hitchcock, who made a manorial house on his large estate in Millbrook, New York, available to Leary as new home and headquarters. Millbrook was also the home of another foundation for the psychedelic, transcendental way of life, the Castalia Foundation.

On a trip to India in 1965 Leary was converted to Hinduism. In the following year he founded a religious community, the League for Spiritual Discovery, whose initials give the abbreviation "LSD."

Leary's proclamation to youth, condensed in his famous slogan "Turn on, tune in, drop out!", became a central dogma of the hippie movement. Leary is one of the founding fathers of the hippie cult. The last of these three precepts, "drop out," was the challenge to escape from bourgeois life, to turn one's back on society, to give up school, studies, and employment, and to dedicate oneself wholly to the true inner universe, the study of one's own nervous system, after one has turned on with LSD. This challenge above all went beyond the psychological and religious domain to assume social and political significance. It is therefore understandable that Leary not only became the *enfant terrible* of the university and among his academic colleagues in psychology and psychiatry, but also earned the wrath of the political authorities. He was, therefore, placed under surveillance, followed, and ultimately locked in prison. The high sentences—ten years' imprisonment each for convictions in Texas and California concerning possession of LSD and marijuana, and conviction (later overturned) with a sentence of thirty years' imprisonment for marijuana smuggling—show that the punishment of these offenses was only a pretext: the real aim was to put under lock and key the seducer and instigator of youth, who could not otherwise be prosecuted. On the night of 13–14 September 1970, Leary managed to escape from the California prison in San Luis Obispo. On a detour from Algeria, where he made contact with Eldridge Cleaver, a leader of the Black Panther movement living there in exile, Leary came to Switzerland and there petitioned for political asylum.

Meeting with Timothy Leary

Dr. Leary lived with his wife, Rosemary, in the resort town Villars-sur-Ollon in western Switzerland. Through the intercession of Dr. Mastronardi, Dr. Leary's lawyer, contact was established between us. On 3 September 1971, I met Dr. Leary in the railway station snack bar in Lausanne. The greeting was cordial, a symbol of our fateful relationship through LSD. Leary was medium-sized, slender, resiliently active, his brown face surrounded with slightly curly hair mixed with gray, youthful, with bright, laughing eyes. This gave Leary somewhat the mark of a tennis champion rather than that of a former Harvard lecturer. We traveled by automobile to Buchillons, where in the arbor of the restaurant A la Grande Forêt, over a meal of fish and a glass of white wine, the dialogue between the father and the apostle of LSD finally began.

77

I voiced my regret that the investigations with LSD and psilocybin at Harvard University, which had begun promisingly, had degenerated to such an extent that their continuance in an academic milieu became impossible.

My most serious remonstrance to Leary, however, concerned the propagation of LSD use among juveniles. Leary did not attempt to refute my opinions about the particular dangers of LSD for youth. He maintained, however, that I was unjustified in reproaching him for the seduction of immature persons to drug consumption, because teenagers in the United States, with regard to information and life experience, were comparable to adult Europeans. Maturity, with satiation and intellectual stagnation, would be reached very early in the United States. For that reason, he deemed the LSD experience significant, useful, and enriching, even for people still very young in years.

In this conversation, I further objected to the great publicity that Leary sought for his LSD and psilocybin investigations, since he had invited reporters from daily papers and magazines to his experiments and had mobilized radio and television. Emphasis was thereby placed on publicity rather than on objective information. Leary defended this publicity program because he felt it had been his fateful historic role to make LSD known worldwide. The overwhelmingly positive effects of such dissemination, above all among America's younger generation, would make any trifling injuries, any regrettable accidents as a result of improper use of LSD, unimportant in comparison, a small price to pay.

During this conversation, I ascertained that one did Leary an injustice by indiscriminately describing him as a drug apostle. He made a sharp distinction between psychedelic drugs—LSD, psilocybin, mescaline, hashish—of whose salutary effects he was persuaded, and the addicting narcotics morphine, heroin, etc., against whose use he repeatedly cautioned.

My impression of Dr. Leary in this personal meeting was that of a charming personage, convinced of his mission, who defended his opinions with humor yet uncompromisingly; a man who truly soared high in the clouds pervaded by beliefs in the wondrous effects of psychedelic drugs and the optimism resulting therefrom, and thus a man who tended to underrate or completely overlook practical difficulties, unpleasant facts, and dangers. Leary also showed carelessness regarding charges and dangers that concerned his own person, as his further path in life emphatically showed.

During his Swiss sojourn, I met Leary by chance once more, in February 1972, in Basel, on the occasion of a visit by Michael Horowitz, curator of the Fitz Hugh Ludlow Memorial Library in San Francisco, a library specializing in drug literature. We traveled together to my house in the country near Burg, where we resumed our conversation of the previous September. Leary appeared fidgety and detached, probably owing to a momentary indisposition, so that our discussions were less productive this time. That was my last meeting with Dr. Leary.

He left Switzerland at the end of the year, having separated from his wife, Rosemary, now accompanied by his new friend Joanna Harcourt-Smith. After a short stay in Austria, where he assisted in a documentary film about heroin, Leary and friend traveled to Afghanistan. At the airport in Kabul he was apprehended by agents of the American secret service and brought back to the San Luis Obispo prison in California.

After nothing had been heard from Leary for a long time, his name again appeared in the daily papers in summer 1975 with the announcement of a parole and early release from prison. But he was not set free until early in 1976. I learned from his friends that he was now occupied with psychological problems of space travel and with the exploration of cosmic relationships between the human nervous system and interstellar space—that is, with problems whose study would bring him no further difficulties on the part of governmental authorities.

Travels in the Universe of the Soul

Thus the Islamic scholar Dr. Rudolf Gelpke entitled his accounts of self-experiments with LSD and psilocybin, which appeared in the publication *Antaios*, for January 1962, and this title could also be used for the following descriptions of LSD experiments. LSD trips and the space flights of the astronauts are comparable in many respects. Both enterprises require very careful preparations, as far as measures for safety as well as objectives are concerned, in order to minimize dangers and to derive the most valuable results possible. The astronauts cannot remain in space nor the LSD experimenters in transcendental spheres, they have to return to earth and everyday reality, where the newly acquired experiences must be evaluated.

The following reports were selected in order to demonstrate how varied the experiences of LSD inebriation can be. The particular motivation for undertaking the experiments was also decisive in their selection. Without exception, this selection involves only reports by persons who have tried LSD not simply out of curiosity or as a sophisticated pleasure drug, but who rather experimented with it in the quest for expanded possibilities of experience of the inner and outer world; who attempted, with the help of this drug key, to unlock new "doors of perception" (William Blake); or, to continue with the comparison chosen by Rudolf Gelpke, who employed LSD to surmount the force of gravity of space and time in the accustomed world view, in order to arrive thereby at new outlooks and understandings in the "universe of the soul."

The first two of the following research records are taken from the previously cited report by Rudolf Gelpke in *Antaios*.

Dance of the Spirits in the Wind

(0.075 mg LSD on 23 June 1961, 13:00 hours)

After I had ingested this dose, which could be considered average, I conversed very animatedly with a professional colleague until approximately 14:00 hours. Following this, I proceeded alone to the Werthmüller bookstore where the drug now began to act most unmistakably. I discerned, above all, that the subjects of the books in which I rummaged peacefully in the back of the shop were indifferent to me, whereas random details of my surroundings suddenly stood out strongly, and somehow appeared to be "meaningful." . . . Then, after some ten minutes, I was discovered by a married couple known to me, and had to let myself become involved in a conversation with them that, I admit, was by no means pleasant to me, though not really painful either. I listened to the conversation (even to myself) "as from far away." The things that were discussed (the conversation dealt with Persian stories that I had translated) "belonged to another world": a world about which I could indeed express myself (I had, after all, recently still inhabited it myself and remembered the "rules of the game"!), but to which I no longer possessed any emotional connection. My interest in it was obliterated—only I did not dare to let myself observe that.

After I managed to dismiss myself, I strolled farther through the city to the marketplace. I had no "visions," saw and heard everything as usual, and yet everything was also altered in an indescribable way; "imperceptible glassy walls" everywhere. With every step that I took, I became more and more like an automaton. It especially struck me that I seemed to lose control over my facial musculature—I was convinced that my face was grown stiff, completely expressionless, empty, slack and masklike. The only reason I could still walk and put myself in motion, was because I remembered that, and how I had "earlier" gone and moved myself. But the farther back the recollection went, the more uncertain I became. I remember that my own hands somehow were in my way: I put them in my pockets, let them dangle, entwined them behind my back . . . as some burdensome objects, which must be dragged around with us and which no one knows quite how to stow away. I had the same reaction concerning my whole body. I no longer knew why it was there, and where I should go with it. All sense for decisions of that kind had been lost. They could only be reconstructed laboriously, taking a detour through memories from the past. It took a struggle of this kind to enable me to cover the short distance from the marketplace to my home, which I reached at about 15:10.

In no way had I had the feeling of being inebriated. What I experienced was rather a gradual mental extinction. It was not at all frightening; but I can imagine that in the transition to certain mental disturbances—naturally dispersed over a greater interval—a very similar process happens: as long as the recollection of the former individual existence in the human world is still present, the patient who has become unconnected can still (to some extent) find his way about in the world: later, however, when the memories fade and ultimately die out, he completely loses this ability.

Shortly after I had entered my room, the "glassy stupor" gave way. I sat down, with a view out of a window, and was at once enraptured: the window was opened wide, the diaphanous gossamer curtains, on the other hand, were drawn, and now a mild wind from the outside played with these veils and with the silhouettes of potted plants and leafy tendrils on the sill behind, which the sunlight delineated on the curtains breathing in the breeze. This spectacle captivated me completely. I "sank" into it, saw only this gentle and incessant waving and rocking of the plant shadows in the sun and the wind. I knew what "it" was, but I sought after the name for it, after the formula, after the "magic word" that I knew—and already I had it: *Totentanz,* the dance of the dead. . . . This was what the wind and the light were showing me on the screen of gossamer. Was it frightening? Was I afraid? Perhaps—at first. But then a great cheerfulness infiltrated me, and I heard the music of silence, and even my soul danced with the redeemed shadows to the whistle of the wind. Yes, I understood: this is the curtain, and this curtain itself IS the secret, the "ultimate" that it concealed. Why, therefore, tear it up? He who does that only tears up himself. Because "there behind," behind the curtain, is "nothing.". . .

Polyp from the Deep

(0.150 mg LSD on 15 April 1961, 9:15 hours)

Beginning of the effect already after about 30 minutes with strong inner agitation, trembling hands, skin chills, taste of metal on the palate.

10:00: The environment of the room transforms itself into phosphorescent waves, running hither from the feet even through my body. The skin—and above all the toes—is as electrically charged; a still constantly growing excitement hinders all clear thoughts. . . .

10:20: I lack the words to describe my current condition. It is as if an "other" complete stranger were seizing possession of me bit by bit. Have greatest trouble writing ("inhibited" or "uninhibited"?—I don't know!).

This sinister process of an advancing self-estrangement aroused in me the feeling of powerlessness, of being helplessly delivered up. Around 10:30, through closed eyes I saw innumerable, self-intertwining threads on a red background. A sky as heavy as lead appeared to press down on everything; I felt my ego compressed in itself, and I felt like a withered dwarf. . . . Shortly before 13:00 I escaped the more and more oppressing atmosphere of the company in the studio, in which we only hindered one another reciprocally from unfolding completely into the inebriation. I sat down in a small, empty room, on the floor, with my back to the wall, and saw through the only window on the narrow frontage opposite me a bit of gray-white cloudy sky. This, like the whole environment in general, appeared to be hopelessly normal at this moment. I was dejected, and my self seemed so repulsive and hateful to me that I had not dared (and on this day even had actually repeatedly desperately avoided) to look in a mirror or in the face of another person. I very much wished this inebriation were finally finished, but it still had my body totally in its possession. I imagined that I perceived, deep within its stubborn oppressive weight, how it held my limbs surrounded with a hundred polyp arms—yes, I actually experienced this in a mysterious rhythm; electrified contacts, as of a real, indeed imperceptible, but sinister omnipresent being, which I addressed with a loud voice, reviled, bid, and challenged to open combat. "It is only the projection of evil in your self," another voice assured me. "It is your soul monster!" This perception was like a flashing sword. It passed through me with redeeming sharpness. The polyp arms fell away from me—as if cut through—and simultaneously the hitherto dull and gloomy gray-white of the sky behind the open window suddenly scintillated like sunlit water. As I stared at it so enchanted, it changed (for me!) to real water: a subterranean spring overran me, which had ruptured there all at once and now boiled up toward me, wanted to become a storm, a lake, an ocean, with millions and millions of drops—and on all of these drops, on every single one of them, the light danced. . . . As the room, window, and sky came back into my consciousness (it was 13:25 hours), the inebriation was certainly not at an end—not yet—but its rearguard, which passed by me during the ensuing two hours, very much resembled the rainbow that follows the storm.

Both the estrangement from the environment and the estrangement from the individual body, experienced in both of the preceding experiments described by Gelpke—as well as the feeling of an alien being, a demon, seizing possession of oneself—are features of LSD inebriation that, in spite of all the other diversity and variability of the experience, are cited in most research reports. I have already described the possession by the LSD demon as an uncanny experience in my first planned self-experiment. Anxiety and terror then affected me especially strongly, because at that time I had no way of knowing that the demon would again release his victim.

The adventures described in the following report, by a painter, belong to a completely different type of LSD experience. This artist visited me in order to obtain my opinion about how the experience under LSD should be understood and interpreted. He feared that the profound transformation of his personal life, which had resulted from his experiment with LSD, could rest on a mere delusion. My explanation—that LSD, as a biochemical agent, only triggered his visions but had not created them and that these visions rather originated from his own soul—gave him confidence in the meaning of his transformation.

LSD Experience of a Painter

. . . Therefore I traveled with Eva to a solitary mountain valley. Up there in nature, I thought it would be particularly beautiful with Eva. Eva was young and attractive. Twenty years older than she, I was already in the middle of life. Despite the sorrowful consequences that I had experienced previously, as a result of erotic escapades, despite the pain and the disappointments that I inflicted on those who loved me and had believed in me, I was drawn again with irresistible power to this adventure, to Eva, to her youth. I was under the spell of this girl. Our affair indeed was only beginning, but I felt this seductive power more strongly than ever before. I knew that I could no longer resist. For the second time in my life I was again ready to desert my family, to give up my position, to break all bridges. I wanted to hurl myself uninhibitedly into this lustful inebriation with Eva. She was life, youth. Over again it cried out in me, again and again to drain the cup of lust and life until the last drop, until death and perdition. Let the Devil fetch me later on! I had indeed long ago done away with God and the Devil. They were for me only human inventions, which came to be utilized by a skeptical, unscrupulous minority, in order to suppress and exploit a believing, naive majority. I wanted to have nothing to do with this mendacious social moral. To enjoy, at all costs, I wished to enjoy *et après nous le déluge.* "What is wife to me, what is child to me—let them go begging, if they are hungry." I also perceived the institution of marriage as a social lie. The marriage of my parents and marriages of my acquaintances seemed to confirm that sufficiently for me. Couples remained together because it was more convenient; they were accustomed to it, and "yes, if it weren't for the children . . ." Under the pretense of a good marriage, each tormented the other emotionally, to the point of rashes and stomach ulcers, or each went his own way. Everything in me rebelled against the thought of having to love only one and the same woman a life long. I frankly perceived that as repugnant and unnatural. Thus stood my inner disposition on that portentous summer evening at the mountain lake.

At seven o'clock in the evening both of us took a moderately strong dose of LSD, some 0.1 milligrams. Then we strolled along about the lake and then sat on the bank. We threw stones in the water and watched the forming wave circles. We felt a slight inner restlessness. Around eight o'clock we entered the hotel lounge and ordered tea and sandwiches. Some guests still sat there, telling jokes and laughing loudly. They winked at us. Their eyes sparkled strangely. We felt strange and distant and had the feeling that they would notice something in us. Outside it slowly became dark. We decided only reluctantly to go to our hotel room. A street without lights led along the black lake to the distant guest house. As I switched on the light, the granite staircase, leading from the shore road to the house, appeared to flame up from step to step. Eva quivered all at once, frightened. "Hellish" went through my mind, and all of a sudden horror passed through my limbs, and I knew: now it's going to turn out badly. From afar, from the village, a clock struck nine.

Scarcely were we in our room, when Eva threw herself on the bed and looked at me with wide eyes. It was not in the least possible to think of love. I sat down on the edge of the bed and held both of Eva's hands. Then came the terror. We sank into a deep, indescribable horror, which neither of us understood.

"Look in my eyes, look at me," I implored Eva, yet again and again her gaze was averted from me, and then she cried out loud in terror and trembled all over her body. There was no way out. Outside was only gloomy night and the deep, black lake. In the public house all the lights were extinguished; the people had probably gone to sleep. What would they have said if they could see us now? Possibly they would summon the police, and then everything would become still much worse. A drug scandal—intolerable agonizing thoughts.

We could no longer move from the spot. We sat there surrounded by four wooden walls whose board joints shone infernally. It became more unbearable all the time. Suddenly the door was opened and "something dreadful" entered. Eva cried out wildly and hid herself under the bed covers. Once again a cry. The horror under the covers was yet worse. "Look straight in my eyes!" I called to her, but she rolled her eyes back and forth as though out of her mind. She is becoming insane, I realized. In desperation I seized her by the hair so that she could no longer turn her face away from me. I saw dreadful fear in her eyes. Everything around us was hostile and threatening, as if everything wanted to attack us in the next moment. You must protect Eva, you must bring her through until morning, then the effects will discontinue, I said to myself. Then again, however, I plunged into nameless horror. There was no more time or reason; it seemed as if this condition would never end.

The objects in the room were animated to caricatures; everything on all sides sneered scornfully. I saw Eva's yellow-black striped shoes, which I had found so stimulating, appearing as two large, evil wasps crawling on the floor. The water piping above the washbasin changed to a dragon head, whose eyes, the two water taps, observed me malevolently. My first name, George, came into my mind, and all at once I felt like Knight

George, who must fight for Eva.

Eva's cries tore me from these thoughts. Bathed in perspiration and trembling, she fastened herself to me. "I am thirsty," she moaned. With great effort, without releasing Eva's hand, I succeeded in getting a glass of water for her. But the water seemed slimy and viscous, was poisonous, and we could not quench our thirst with it. The two night-table lamps glowed with a strange brightness, in an infernal light. The clock struck twelve.

This is hell, I thought. There is indeed no Devil and no demons, and yet they were perceptible in us, filled up the room, and tormented us with unimaginable terror. Imagination, or not? Hallucinations, projections?—insignificant questions when confronted with the reality of fear that was fixed in our bodies and shook us: the fear alone, it existed. Some passages from Huxley's book *The Doors of Perception* came to me and brought me brief comfort. I looked at Eva, at this whimpering, horrified being in her torment, and felt great remorse and pity. She had become strange to me; I scarcely recognized her any longer. She wore a fine golden chain around her neck with the medallion of the Virgin Mary. It was a gift from her younger brother. I noticed how a benevolent, comforting radiation, which was connected with pure love, emanated from this necklace. But then the terror broke loose again, as if to our final destruction. I needed my whole strength to constrain Eva. Loudly I heard the electrical meter ticking weirdly outside of the door, as if it wanted to make a most important, evil, devastating announcement to me in the next moment. Disdain, derision, and malignity again whispered out of all nooks and crevices. There, in the midst of this agony, I perceived the ringing of cowbells from afar as a wonderful, promising music. Yet soon it became silent again, and renewed fear and dread once again set in. As a drowning man hopes for a rescuing plank, so I wished that the cows would yet again want to draw near the house. But everything remained quiet, and only the threatening tick and hum of the current meter buzzed round us like an invisible, malevolent insect.

Morning finally dawned. With great relief I noticed how the chinks in the window shutters lit up. Now I could leave Eva to herself; she had quieted down. Exhausted, she closed her eyes and fell asleep. Shocked and deeply sad, I still sat on the edge of the bed. Gone was my pride and self-assurance; all that remained of me was a small heap of misery. I examined myself in the mirror and started: I had become ten years older in the course of the night. Downcast, I stared at the light of the night-table lamp with the hideous shade of intertwined plastic cords. All at once the light seemed to become brighter, and in the plastic cords it began to sparkle and to twinkle; it glowed like diamonds and gems of all colors, and an overwhelming feeling of happiness welled up in me. All at once, lamp, room, and Eva disappeared, and I found myself in a wonderful, fantastic landscape. It was comparable to the interior of an immense Gothic church nave, with infinitely many columns and Gothic arches. These consisted, however, not of stone, but rather of crystal. Bluish, yellowish, milky, and clearly transparent crystal columns surrounded me like trees in an open forest. Their points and arches became lost in dizzying heights. A bright light appeared before my inner eye, and a wonderful, gentle voice spoke to me out of the light. I did not hear it with my external ear, but rather perceived it, as if it were clear thoughts that arise in one.

I realized that in the horror of the passing night I had experienced my own individual condition: selfishness. My egotism had kept me separated from mankind and had led me to inner isolation. I had loved only myself, not my neighbor; loved only the gratification that the other offered me. The world had existed only for the satisfaction of my greed. I had become tough, cold, and cynical. Hell, therefore, had signified that: egotism and lovelessness. Therefore everything had seemed strange and unconnected to me, so scornful and threatening. Amid flowing tears, I was enlightened with the knowledge that true love means surrender of selfishness and that it is not desires but rather selfless love that forms the bridge to the heart of our fellow man. Waves of ineffable happiness flowed through my body. I had experienced the grace of God. But how could it be possible that it was radiating toward me, particularly out of this cheap lampshade? Then the inner voice answered: God is in everything.

The experience at the mountain lake has given me the certainty that beyond the ephemeral, material world there also exists an imperishable, spiritual reality, which is our true home. I am now on my way home.

For Eva everything remained just a bad dream. We broke up a short time thereafter.

The following notes kept by a twenty-five-year-old advertising agent are contained in *The LSD Story* by John Cashman (Fawcett Publications, Greenwich, Conn., 1966). They were included in this selection of LSD reports, along with the preceding example, because the progression that they describe—from terrifying visions to extreme euphoria, a kind of death-rebirth cycle—is characteristic of many LSD experiments.

A Joyous Song of Being

My first experience with LSD came at the home of a close friend who served as my guide. The surroundings were comfortably familiar and relaxing. I took two ampuls (200 micrograms) of LSD mixed in half a glass of distilled water. The experience lasted for close to eleven hours, from 8 o'clock on a Saturday evening until very nearly 7 o'clock the next morning. I have no firm point of comparison, but I am positive that no saint ever saw more glorious or joyously beautiful visions or experienced a more blissful state of transcendence. My powers to convey the miracles are shabby and far too inadequate to the task at hand. A sketch, and an artless one at that, must suffice where only the hand of a great master working from a complete palette could do justice to the subject. I must apologize

94

for my own limitations in this feeble attempt to reduce the most remarkable experience of my life to mere words. My superior smile at the fumbling, halting attempts of others in their attempts to explain the heavenly visions to me has been transformed into a knowing smile of a conspirator—the common experience requires no words.

My first thought after drinking the LSD was that it was having absolutely no effect. They had told me thirty minutes would produce the first sensation, a tingling of the skin. There was no tingling. I commented on this and was told to relax and wait. For the lack of anything else to do I stared at the dial light of the table radio, nodding my head to a jazz piece I did not recognize. I think it was several minutes before I realized that the light was changing color kaleidoscopically with the different pitch of the musical sounds, bright reds and yellows in the high register, deep purple in the low. I laughed. I had no idea when it had started. I simply knew it had. I closed my eyes, but the colored notes were still there. I was overcome by the remarkable brilliance of the colors. I tried to talk, to explain what I was seeing, the vibrant and luminous colors. Somehow it didn't seem important. With my eyes open, the radiant colors flooded the room, folding over on top of one another in rhythm with the music. Suddenly I was aware that the colors *were* the music. The discovery did not seem startling. Values, so cherished and guarded, were becoming unimportant. I wanted to talk about the colored music, but I couldn't. I was reduced to uttering one-syllable words while polysyllabic impressions tumbled through my mind with the speed of light.

The dimensions of the room were changing, now sliding into a fluttering diamond shape, then straining into an oval shape as if someone were pumping air into the room, expanding it to the bursting point. I was having trouble focusing on objects. They would melt into fuzzy masses of nothing or sail off into space, self-propelled, slow-motion trips that were of acute interest to me. I tried to check the time on my watch, but I was unable to focus on the hands. I thought of asking for the time, but the thought passed. I was too busy seeing and listening. The sounds were exhilarating, the sights remarkable. I was completely entranced. I have no idea how long this lasted. I do know the egg came next.

The egg, large, pulsating, and a luminous green, was there before I actually saw it. I *sensed* it was there. It hung suspended about halfway between where I sat and the far wall. I was intrigued by the beauty of the egg. At the same time I was afraid it would drop to the floor and break. I didn't want the egg to break. It seemed most important that the egg should not break. But even as I thought of this, the egg slowly dissolved and revealed a great multihued flower that was like no flower I have ever seen. Its incredibly exquisite petals opened on the room, spraying indescribable colors in every direction. I felt the colors and *heard* them as they played across my body, cool and warm, reedlike and tinkling.

The first tinge of apprehension came later

when I saw the center of the flower slowly
eating away at the petals, a black, shiny center
that appeared to be formed by the backs of a
thousand ants. It ate away the petals at an
agonizingly slow pace. I wanted to scream for it
to stop or to hurry up. I was pained by the
gradual disappearance of the beautiful petals
as if being swallowed by an insidious disease.
Then in a flash of insight I realized to my horror
that the black thing was actually devouring
me. I was the flower and this foreign, creeping
thing was eating *me*!

I shouted or screamed, I really don't
remember. I was too full of fear and loathing. I
heard my guide say: "Easy now. Just go with it.
Don't fight it. Go with it." I tried, but the
hideous blackness caused such repulsion that I
screamed: "I can't! For God's sake help me!
Help me!" The voice was soothing, reassuring:
"Let it come. Everything is all right. Don't
worry. Go with it. Don't fight."

I felt myself dissolving into the terrifying
apparition, my body melting in waves into the
core of blackness, my mind stripped of ego and
life and, yes even death. In one great crystal
instant I realized that I was immortal. I asked
the question: "Am I dead?" But the question
had no meaning. Meaning was meaningless.
Suddenly there was white light and the
shimmering beauty of unity. There was light
everywhere, white light with a clarity beyond
description. I was dead and I was born and the
exultation was pure and holy. My lungs were
bursting with the joyful song of being. There
was unity and life and the exquisite love that
filled my being was unbounded. My awareness

was acute and complete. I saw God and the devil and all the saints and I knew the truth. I felt myself flowing into the cosmos, levitated beyond all restraint, liberated to swim in the blissful radiance of the heavenly visions.

I wanted to shout and sing of miraculous new life and sense and form, of the joyous beauty and the whole mad ecstasy of loveliness. I knew and understood all there is to know and understand. I was immortal, wise beyond wisdom, and capable of love, of all loves. Every atom of my body and soul had seen and felt God. The world was warmth and goodness. There was no time, no place, no me. There was only cosmic harmony. It was all there in the white light. With every fiber of my being I knew it was so.

I embraced the enlightenment with complete abandonment. As the experience receded I longed to hold onto it and tenaciously fought against the encroachment of the realities of time and place. For me, the realities of our limited existence were no longer valid. I had seen the ultimate realities and there would be no others. As I was slowly transported back to the tyranny of clocks and schedules and petty hatreds, I tried to talk of my trip, my enlightenment, the horrors, the beauty, all of it. I must have been babbling like an idiot. My thoughts swirled at a fantastic rate, but the words couldn't keep pace. My guide smiled and told me he understood.

The preceding collection of reports on "travels in the universe of the soul," even though they encompass such dissimilar experiences, are still not able to establish a complete picture of the broad spectrum of all possible reactions to LSD, which extends from the most sublime spiritual, religious, and mystical experiences, down to gross psychosomatic disturbances. Cases of LSD sessions have been described in which the stimulation of fantasy and of visionary experience, as expressed in the LSD reports assembled here, is completely absent, and the experimenter was for the whole time in a state of ghastly physical and mental discomfort, or even felt severely ill.

Reports about the modification of sexual experience under the influence of LSD are also contradictory. Since stimulation of all sensory perception is an essential feature of LSD effects, the sensual orgy of sexual intercourse can undergo unimaginable enhancements. Cases have also been described, however, in which LSD led not to the anticipated erotic paradise, but rather to a purgatory or even to the hell of frightful extinction of every perception and to a lifeless vacuum.

Such a variety and contradiction of reactions to a drug is found only in LSD and the related hallucinogens. The explanation for this lies in the complexity and variability of the conscious and subconscious minds of people, which LSD is able to penetrate and to bring to life as experienced reality.

Rye infected with sclerotia of ergot *(Claviceps purpurea)*.

Inset: St. Anthony, patron saint of ergotism victims, in an icon from the Staatliche Graphische Sammlung, Munich.

Above: Micrograph of crystals of LSD.

Below: Extract from the author's laboratory journal concerning preparation of LSD tartrate and the first planned self-experiment.

Above: Pre-Columbian stone mushroom icon of a young woman bending over a *metate*. Pre-classic Mayan artifact (ca. 1000-500 B.C.) from the collection of Hans Namuth.

Below: Two views of a pre-Columbian stone mushroom icon from classic Mayan culture (ca. 300-600 A.D.). From collection of the Rietberg Museum, Zurich.

Above: The Mazatec shaman María Sabina ingesting *Psilocybe caerulescens* during a *velada* (vigil) in Huavtla de Jimenez, Oaxaca.

Below: María Sabina invokes the power of the wondrous mushrooms.

Above: Artificial culture of *Psilocybe mexicana*, from which psilocybin and psilocin were first isolated by the author in the Sandoz laboratories.

Below: Micrographs of crystals of psilocybin and psilocin from methanol.

Above: Turbina corymbosa, known as coaxihuitl (snake plant) to the Aztecs; source of entheogenic ololiuhqui seeds.

Below: The first illustration of coaxihuitl, from Francisco Hernández, *Rerum Medicarum Novae Hispaniae Thesaurus seu Plantarum, Animalium, Mineralium Mexicanorum Historia,* published in Rome in 1651.

De OLILIVHQVI, *feu planta orbicularium foliorum.* Cap. XIV.

OLILIVHQVI, quam *Coaxihuitl*, feu herbam Serpentis alij vocant, volubilis herba eft, folia viridia ferens, tenuia, cordis figura. caules teretes, virides, tenuefq; . flores albos, & longiufculos. femen rotundum fimile Coriandro, vnde nomen. radices fibris fimiles. calida quarto ordine planta eft. luem Gallicam curat. dolores è frigore ortos fedat. flatum, ac præter naturam tumores difcutit. puluis refina mixtus pellit frigus. luxatis aut fractis offibus, & lumbis fœminarum laxis, aucto robore mirum auxiliatur in modum. S eminis etiam eft vfus in medicina, quod tritum, ac deuoratum, illitumq; capiti, & fronti, cum lacte & *Chilli*, fertur morbis oculorum mederi. deuoratum verò, venerem excitat. Acri eft fapore, & temperie, veluti & planta eius, impensè calida. Indorum facrifici cum videri volebant verfari cum Superis, ac refpófa accipere ab eis, ea vefcebátur planta, vt defiperent, milleq; phantafmata, & dæmonú obuerfátium effigies circumfpectarent. qua in re Solano maniaco Diofcoridis fimilis fortaffe alicui videri poffit.

6

The Mexican Relatives
of LSD

The Sacred Mushroom Teonanácatl

Late in 1956 a notice in the daily paper caught my interest. Among some Indians in southern Mexico, American researchers had discovered mushrooms that were eaten in religious ceremonies and that produced an inebriated condition accompanied by hallucinations.

Since, outside of the mescaline cactus found also in Mexico, no other drug was known at the time that, like LSD, produced hallucinations, I would have liked to establish contact with these researchers, in order to learn details about these hallucinogenic mushrooms. But there were no names and addresses in the short newspaper article, so that it was impossible to get further information. Nevertheless, the mysterious mushrooms, whose chemical investigation would be a tempting problem, stayed in my thoughts from then on.

As it later turned out, LSD was the reason that these mushrooms found their way into my laboratory, without my assistance, at the beginning of the following year.

Through the mediation of Dr. Yves Dunant, at the time director of the Paris branch of Sandoz, an inquiry came to the pharmaceutical research management in Basel from Professor Roger Heim, director of the Laboratoire de Cryptogamie of the Muséum National d'Histoire Naturelle in Paris, asking whether we were interested in carrying out the chemical investigation of the Mexican hallucinogenic mushrooms. With great joy I declared myself ready to begin this work in my department, in the laboratories for natural product research. That was to be my link to the exciting investigations of the Mexican sacred mushrooms, which were already broadly advanced in the ethnomycological and botanical aspects.

For a long time the existence of these magic mushrooms had remained an enigma. The history of their rediscovery is presented at first hand in the magnificent two-volume standard work of ethnomycology, *Mushrooms, Russia and History* (Pantheon Books, New York, 1957), for the authors, the American researchers Valentina Pavlovna Wasson and her husband, R. Gordon Wasson, played a decisive role in this rediscovery. The following descriptions of the fascinating history of these mushrooms are taken from the Wassons' book.

The first written evidence of the use of inebriating mushrooms on festival occasions, or in the course of religious ceremonies and magically oriented healing practices, is found among the Spanish chroniclers and naturalists of the sixteenth century, who entered the country soon after the conquest of Mexico by Hernán Cortés. The most important of these witnesses is the Franciscan friar Bernardino de Sahagún, who mentions the magic mushrooms and describes their effects and their use in several passages of his famous historical work, *Historia General de las Cosas de Nueva España*, written between the years 1529 and 1590. Thus he describes, for example, how merchants celebrated the return home from a successful business trip with a mushroom party:

> Coming at the very first, at the time of feasting, they ate mushrooms when, as they said, it was the hour of the blowing of the flutes. Not yet did they partake of food; they drank only chocolate during the night. And they ate mushrooms with honey. When already the mushrooms were taking effect, there was dancing, there was weeping. . . . Some saw in a vision that they would die in war. Some saw in a vision that they would be devoured by wild beasts. . . . Some saw in a vision that they would become rich, wealthy. Some saw in a vision that they would buy slaves, would become slave owners. Some saw in a vision that they would commit adultery [and so] would have their heads bashed in, would be stoned to death. . . . Some saw in a vision that they would perish in the water. Some saw in a vision that they would pass to tranquility in death. Some saw in a vision that they would fall from the housetop, tumble to their death. . . . All such things they saw. . . . And when [the effects of] the mushroom ceased, they conversed with one another, spoke of what they had seen in the vision.

In a publication from the same period, Diego Durán, a Dominican friar, reported that inebriating mushrooms were eaten at the great festivity on the occasion of the accession to the throne of Moctezuma II, the famed emperor of the Aztecs, in the year 1502. A passage in the seventeenth-century chronicle of Don Jacinto de la Serna refers to the use of these mushrooms in a religious framework:

> And what happened was that there had come to [the village] an Indian . . . and his name was Juan Chichiton . . . and he had brought the red-colored mushrooms that are gathered in the uplands, and with them he had committed a great idolatry. . . . In the house where everyone had gathered on the occasion of a saint's feast . . . the *teponastli* [an Aztec percussion instrument] was playing and singing was going on the whole night through. After most of the night had passed, Juan Chichiton, who was the priest for that solumn rite, to all of those present at the fiesta gave the mushrooms to eat, after the manner of Communion, and gave them *pulque* to drink . . . so that they all went out of their heads, a shame it was to see.

In Nahuatl, the language of the Aztecs, these mushrooms were described as *teonanáctl*, which can be translated as "sacred mushroom."

There are indications that ceremonial use of such mushrooms reaches far back into pre-Columbian times. So-called mushroom stones have been found in El Salvador, Guatemala, and the contiguous mountainous districts of Mexico. These are stone sculptures in the form of pileate mushroom, on whose stem the face or the form of a god or an animallike demon is carved. Most are about 30 cm high. The oldest examples, according to archaeologists, date back to before 500 B.C.

R. G. Wasson argues, quite convincingly, that there

is a connection between these mushroom stones and *teonanácatl*. If true, this means that the mushroom cult, the magico-medicinal and religious-ceremonial use of the magic mushrooms, is more than two thousand years old.

To the Christian missionaries, the inebriating, vision- and hallucination-producing effects of these mushrooms seemed to be Devil's work. They therefore tried, with all the means in their power, to extirpate their use. But they succeeded only partially, for the Indians have continued secretly down to our time to utilize the mushroom *teonanácatl*, which was sacred to them.

Strange to say, the reports in the old chronicles about the use of magic mushrooms remained unnoticed during the following centuries, probably because they were considered products of the imagination of a superstitious age.

All traces of the existence of "sacred mushrooms" were in danger of becoming obliterated once and for all, when, in 1915, an American botanist of repute, Dr. W. E. Safford, in an address before the Botanical Society in Washington and in a scientific publication, advanced the thesis that no such thing as magic mushrooms had ever existed at all: the Spanish chroniclers had taken the mescaline cactus for a mushroom! Even if false, this proposition of Safford's served nevertheless to direct the attention of the scientific world to the riddle of the mysterious mushrooms.

It was the Mexican physician Dr. Blas Pablo Reko who first openly disagreed with Safford's interpretation and who found evidence that mushrooms were still employed in medicinal-religious ceremonies even in our time, in remote districts of the southern mountains of Mexico. But not until the years 1936–38 did the anthropologist Robert J. Weitlaner and Dr. Richard

Evans Schultes, a botanist from Harvard University, find actual mushrooms in that region, which were used there for this ceremonial purpose; and only in 1938 could a group of young American anthropologists, under the direction of Jean Bassett Johnson, attend a secret nocturnal mushroom ceremony for the first time. This was in Huautla de Jiménez, the capital of the Mazatec country, in the State of Oaxaca. But these researchers were only spectators, they were not permitted to partake of the mushrooms. Johnson reported on the experience in a Swedish journal (*Ethnological Studies* 9, 1939).

Then exploration of the magic mushrooms was interrupted. World War II broke out. Schultes, at the behest of the American government, had to occupy himself with rubber production in the Amazon territory, and Johnson was killed after the Allied landing in North Africa.

It was the American researchers, the married couple Dr. Valentina Pavlovna Wasson and her husband, R. Gordon Wasson, who again took up the problem from the ethnographic aspect. R. G. Wasson was a banker, vice-president of the J. P. Morgan Co. in New York. His wife, who died in 1958, was a pediatrician. The Wassons began their work in 1953, in the Mazatec village Huautla de Jiménez, where fifteen years earlier J. B. Johnson and others had established the continued existence of the ancient Indian mushroom cult. They received especially valuable information from an American missionary who had been active there for many years, Eunice V. Pike, member of the Wycliffe Bible Translators. Thanks to her knowledge of the native language and her ministerial association with the inhabitants, Pike had information about the significance of the magic mushrooms that nobody else possessed. During several lengthy sojourns in

Huautla and environs, the Wassons were able to study the present use of the mushrooms in detail and compare it with the descriptions in the old chronicles. This showed that the belief in the "sacred mushrooms" was still prevalent in that region. However, the Indians kept their beliefs a secret from strangers. It took great tact and skill, therefore, to gain the confidence of the indigenous population and to receive insight into this secret domain.

In the modern form of the mushroom cult, the old religious ideas and customs are mingled with Christian ideas and Christian terminology. Thus the mushrooms are often spoken of as the blood of Christ, because they will grow only where a drop of Christ's blood has fallen on the earth. According to another notion, the mushrooms sprout where a drop of saliva from Christ's mouth has moistened the ground, and it is therefore Jesus Christ himself who speaks through the mushrooms.

The mushroom ceremony follows the form of a consultation. The seeker of advice or a sick person or his or her family questions a "wise man" or a "wise woman," a *sabio* or *sabia*, also named *curandero* or *curandera*, in return for a modest payment. *Curandero* can best be translated into English as "healing priest," for his function is that of a physician as well as that of a priest, both being found only rarely in these remote regions. In the Mazatec language the healing priest is called *co-ta-ci-ne*, which means "one who knows." He eats the mushroom in the framework of a ceremony that always takes place at night. The other persons present at the ceremony may sometimes receive mushrooms as well, yet a much greater dose always goes to the *curandero*. The performance is executed with the accompaniment of prayers and entreaties, while the mushrooms are incensed briefly over a basin, in which *copal* (an incense-like resin) is burned. In complete darkness, at times by candlelight, while the others present lie quietly on their straw mats, the *curandero*, kneeling or sitting, prays and sings before a type of altar bearing a crucifix, an image of a saint, or some other object of worship. Under the influence of the sacred mushrooms, the *curandero* counsels in a visionary state, in which even the inactive observers more or less participate. In the monotonous song of the *curandero*, the mushroom *teonanácatl* gives its answers to the questions posed. It says whether the diseased person will live or die, which herbs will effect the cure; it reveals who has killed a specific person, or who has stolen the horse; or it makes known how a distant relative fares, and so forth.

The mushroom ceremony not only has the function of a consulation of the type described, for the Indians it also has a meaning in many respects similar to the Holy Communion for the believing Christian. From many utterances of the natives it could be inferred that they believe that God has given the Indians the sacred mushroom because they are poor and possess no doctors and medicines; and also, because they cannot read, in particular the Bible, God can therefore speak directly to them through the mushroom. The missionary Eunice V. Pike even alluded to the difficulties that result from explaining the Christian message, the written word, to a people who believe they possess a means—the sacred mushrooms of course—to make God's will known to them in a direct, clear manner: yes, the mushrooms permit them to see into heaven and to establish communication with God himself.

The Indians' reverence for the sacred mushrooms is also evident in their belief that they can be eaten only by a "clean" person. "Clean" here means ceremonially clean, and that term among other things includes sexual abstinence at least four days before and after ingestion of the mushrooms. Certain rules must also be observed in gathering the mushrooms. With nonobservance of these commandments, the mushrooms can make the person who eats it insane, or can even kill.

The Wassons had undertaken their first expedition to the Mazatec country in 1953, but not until 1955 did they succeed in overcoming the shyness and reserve of the Mazatec friends they had managed to make, to the point of being admitted as active participants in a mushroom ceremony. R. Gordon Wasson and his companion, the photographer Allan Richardson, were given sacred mushrooms to eat at the end of June 1955, on the occasion of a nocturnal mushroom ceremony. They thereby became in all likelihood the first outsiders, the first whites, ever permitted to take *teonanácatl*.

In the second volume of *Mushrooms, Russia and History*, in enraptured words, Wasson describes how the mushroom seized possession of him completely, although he had tried to struggle against its effects, in order to be able to remain an objective observer. First he saw geometric, colored patterns, which then took on architectural characteristics. Next followed visions of splendid colonnades, palaces of supernatural harmony and magnificence embellished with precious gems, triumphal cars drawn by fabulous creatures as they are known only from mythology, and landscapes of fabulous luster. Detached from the body, the spirit soared timelessly in a realm of fantasy among images of a higher reality and deeper meaning than those of the ordinary, everyday world. The essence of life, the ineffable, seemed to be on the verge of being unlocked, but the ultimate door failed to open.

This experience was the final proof, for Wasson, that the magical powers attributed to the mushrooms actually existed and were not merely superstition.

In order to introduce the mushrooms to scientific research, Wasson had earlier established an association with mycologist Professor Roger Heim of Paris. Accompanying the Wassons on further expeditions into the Mazatec country, Heim conducted the botanical identification of the sacred mushrooms. He showed that they were gilled mushrooms from the family *Strophariaceae*, about a dozen different species not previously described scientifically, the greatest part belonging to the genus *Psilocybe*. Professor Heim also succeeded in cultivating some of the species in the laboratory. The mushroom *Psilocybe mexicana* turned out to be especially suitable for artificial cultivation.

Chemical investigations ran parallel with these botanical studies on the magic mushrooms, with the goal of extracting the hallucinogenically active principle from the mushroom material and preparing it in chemically pure form. Such investigations were carried out at Professor Heim's instigation in the chemical laboratory of the Muséum National d'Histoire Naturelle in Paris, and work teams were occupied with this problem in the United States in the research laboratories of two large pharmaceutical companies: Merck, and Smith, Kline and French. The American laboratories had obtained some of the mushrooms from R. G. Wasson and had gathered others themselves in the Sierra Mazateca.

As the chemical investigations in Paris and in the United States turned out to be ineffectual, Professor Heim addressed this matter to our firm, as mentioned at the beginning of this chapter, because he felt that our experimental experience with LSD, related to the magic mushrooms by similar activity, could be of use in the isolation attempts. Thus it was LSD that showed *teonanácatl* the way into our laboratory.

As director of the department of natural products of the Sandoz pharmaceutical-chemical research laboratories at that time, I wanted to assign the investigation of the magic mushrooms to one of my coworkers. However, nobody showed much eagerness to take on this problem because it was known that LSD and everything connected with it were scarcely popular subjects to the top management. Because the enthusiasm necessary for successful endeavors cannot be commanded, and because the enthusiasm was already present in me as far as this problem was concerned, I decided to conduct the investigation myself.

Some 100 g of dried mushrooms of the species *Psilocybe mexicana*, cultivated by Professor Heim in the laboratory, were available for the beginning of the chemical analysis. My laboratory assistant, Hans Tscherter, who during our decade-long collaboration, had developed into a very capable helper, completely familiar with my manner of work, aided me in the extraction and isolation attempts. Since there were no clues at all concerning the chemical properties of the active principle we sought, the isolation attempts had to be conducted on the basis of the effects of the extract fractions. But none of the various extracts showed an unequivocal effect, either in the mouse or the dog, which could have pointed to the presence of hallucinogenic principles. It therefore became doubtful whether the mushrooms cultivated and dried in Paris were still active at all. That could only be determined by experimenting with this mushroom material on a human being. As in the case of LSD, I made this fundamental experiment myself, since it is not appropriate for researchers to ask anyone else to perform self-experiments that they require for their own investigations, especially if they entail, as in this case, a certain risk.

In this experiment I ate 32 dried specimens of *Psilocybe mexicana*, which together weighed 2.4 g. This amount corresponded to an average dose, according to the reports of Wasson and Heim, as it is used by the *curanderos*. The mushrooms displayed a strong psychic effect, as the following extract from the report on that experiment shows:

Thirty minutes after my taking the mushrooms, the exterior world began to undergo a strange transformation. Everything assumed a Mexican character. As I was perfectly well aware that my knowledge of the Mexican origin of the mushroom would lead me to imagine only Mexican scenery, I tried deliberately to look on my environment as I knew it normally. But all voluntary efforts to look at things in their customary forms and colors proved ineffective. Whether my eyes were closed or open, I saw only Mexican motifs and colors. When the doctor supervising the experiment bent over me to check my blood pressure, he was transformed into an Aztec priest and I would not have been astonished if he had drawn an obsidian knife. In spite of the seriousness of the situation, it amused me to see how the Germanic face of my colleague had acquired a purely Indian expression. At the peak of the intoxication, about 1½ hours after ingestion of the mushrooms, the rush of interior pictures, mostly abstract motifs rapidly changing in shape and color, reached such an alarming degree that I feared that I would be torn into this whirlpool of form and color and would dissolve. After about six hours the dream came to an end. Subjectively, I had no idea how long this condition had lasted. I felt my return to everyday reality to be a happy return from a strange, fantastic but quite real world to an old and familiar home.

This self-experiment showed once again that human beings react much more sensitively than animals to psychoactive substances. We had already reached the same conclusion in experimenting with LSD on animals, as described in an earlier chapter of this book. It was not inactivity of the mushroom material, but rather the deficient reaction capability of the research animals vis-á-vis such a type of active principle, that explained why our extracts had appeared inactive in the mouse and dog.

Because the assay on human subjects was the only test at our disposal for the detection of the active extract fractions, we had no other choice than to perform the testing on ourselves if we wanted to carry on the work and bring it to a successful conclusion. In the self-experiment just described, a strong reaction lasting several hours was produced by 2.4 g dried mushrooms. Therefore, in the sequel we used samples corresponding to only one-third of this amount, namely 0.8 g dried mushrooms. If these samples contained the active principle, they would only provoke a mild effect that impaired the ability to work for a short time, but this effect would still be so distinct that the inactive fractions and those containing the active principle could unequivocally be differentiated from one another. Several coworkers and colleagues volunteered as guinea pigs for this series of tests.

Psilocybin and Psilocin

With the help of this reliable test on human subjects, the active principle could be isolated, concentrated, and transformed into a chemically pure state by means of the newest separation methods. Two new substances, which I named psilocybin and psilocin, were thereby obtained in the form of colorless crystals.

These results were published in March 1958 in the journal *Experientia*, in collaboration with Professor Heim and with my colleagues Dr. A. Brack and Dr. H. Kobel, who had provided greater quantities of mushroom material for these investigations after they had essentially improved the laboratory cultivation of the mushrooms.

Some of my coworkers at the time—Drs. A. J. Frey, H. Ott, T. Petrzilka, and F. Troxler—then participated in the next steps of these investigations, the determination of the chemical structure of psilocybin and psilocin and the subsequent synthesis of these compounds, the results of which were published in the November 1958 issue of *Experientia*. The chemical structures of these mushroom factors deserve special attention in several respects. Psilocybin and psilocin belong, like LSD, to the indole compounds, the biologically important class of substances found in the plant and animal kingdoms. Particular chemical features common to both the mushroom substances and LSD show that psilocybin and psilocin are closely related to LSD, not only with regard to psychic effects but also to their chemical structures. Psilocybin is the phosphoric acid ester of psilocin and, as such, is the first and hitherto only phosphoric-acid-containing indole compound discovered in nature. The phosphoric acid residue does not contribute to the activity, for the phosphoric-acid-free psilocin is just as active as psilocybin, but it makes the molecule more stable. While psilocin is readily decomposed by the oxygen in air, psilocybin is a stable substance.

Psilocybin and psilocin possess a chemical structure very similar to the brain factor serotonin. As was already mentioned in the chapter on animal experiments and biological research, serotonin plays an important role in the chemistry of brain functions. The two mushroom factors, like LSD, block the effects of serotonin in pharmacological experiments on different organs. Other pharmacological properties of psilocybin and psilocin are also similar to those of LSD. The main difference consists in the quantitative activity, in animal as well as human experimentation. The average active dose of psilocybin or psilocin in human beings amounts to 10 mg (0.01 g); accordingly, these two substances are more than 100 times less active than LSD, of which 0.1 mg constitutes a strong dose. Moreover, the effects of the mushroom factors last only four to six hours, much shorter than the effects of LSD (eight to twelve hours).

The total synthesis of psilocybin and psilocin, without the aid of the mushrooms, could be developed into a technical process, which would allow these substances to be produced on a large scale. Synthetic production is more rational and cheaper than extraction from the mushrooms.

Thus with the isolation and synthesis of the active principles, the demystification of the magic mushrooms was accomplished. The compounds whose wondrous effects led the Indians to believe for millennia that a god was residing in the mushrooms had their chemical structures elucidated and could be produced synthetically in flasks.

Just what progress in scientific knowledge was accomplished by natural products research in this case?

Essentially, when all is said and done, we can only say that the mystery of the wondrous effects of *teonanácatl* was reduced to the mystery of the effects of two crystalline substances—since these effects cannot be explained by science either, but can only be described.

A Voyage into the Universe of the Soul with Psilocybin

The relationship between the psychic effects of psilocybin and those of LSD, their visionary-hallucinatory character, is evident in the following report from *Antaios*, of a psilocybin experiment by Dr. Rudolf Gelpke. He has characterized his experiences with LSD and psilocybin, as already mentioned in a previous chapter, as "travels in the universe of the soul."

Where Time Stands Still

(10 mg psilocybin, 6 April 1961, 10:20)

> After ca. 20 minutes, beginning effects: serenity, speechlessness, mild but pleasant dizzy sensation, and "pleasureful deep breathing."
> 10:50 Strong! dizziness, can no longer concentrate . . .
> 10:55 Excited, intensity of colors: everything pink to red.
> 11:05 The world concentrates itself there on the center of the table. Colors very intense.
> 11:10 A divided being, unprecedented—how can I describe this sensation of life? Waves, different selves, must control me.

Immediately after this note I went outdoors, leaving the breakfast table, where I had eaten with Dr. H. and our wives, and lay down on the lawn. The inebriation pushed rapidly to its climax. Although I had firmly resolved to make constant notes, it now seemed to me a complete waste of time, the motion of writing infinitely slow, the possibilities of verbal expression unspeakably paltry—measured by the flood of inner experience that inundated me and threatened to burst me. It seemed to me that 100 years would not be sufficient to describe the fullness of experience of a single minute. At the beginning, optical impressions predominated: I saw with delight the boundless succession of rows of trees in the nearby forest. Then the tattered clouds in the sunny sky rapidly piled up with silent and breathtaking majesty to a superimposition of thousands of layers—heaven on heaven—and I waited then expecting that up there in the next moment something completely powerful, unheard of, not yet existing, would appear or happen—would I behold a god? But only the expectation remained, the presentiment, this hovering, "on the threshold of the ultimate feeling." . . . Then I moved farther away (the proximity of others disturbed me) and lay down in a nook of the garden on a sun-warmed wood pile—my fingers stroked this wood with overflowing, animal-like sensual affection. At the same time I was submerged within myself; it was an absolute climax: a sensation of bliss pervaded me, a contented happiness—I found myself behind my closed eyes in a cavity full of brick-red ornaments, and at the same time in the "center of the universe of consummate calm." I knew everything was good—the cause and origins of everything was good. But at the same moment I also understood the suffering and the loathing, the depression and misunderstanding of ordinary life: there one is never "total," but instead divided, cut in pieces, and split up into the tiny fragments of seconds, minutes, hours, days, weeks, and years: there one is a slave of Moloch time, which devoured one piecemeal; one is condemned to stammering, bungling, and patchwork; one must drag about with oneself the perfection and absolute, the togetherness of all things; the eternal moment of the golden age, this original ground of being—that indeed nevertheless has always endured and will endure forever—there in the weekday of human existence, as a tormenting thorn buried deeply in the soul, as a memorial of a claim never fulfilled, as a fata morgana of a lost and promised paradise; through this feverish dream "present" to a condemned "past" in a clouded "future." I understood. This inebriation was a spaceflight, not of the outer but rather of the inner man, and for a moment I experienced reality from a location that lies somewhere beyond the force of gravity of time.

As I began again to feel this force of gravity, I was childish enough to want to postpone the return by taking a new dose of 6 mg psilocybin at 11:45, and once again 4 mg at 14:30. The effect was trifling, and in any case not worth mentioning.

Mrs. Li Gelpke, an artist, also participated in this series of investigations, taking three self-experiments with LSD and psilocybin. The artist wrote of the drawing she made during the experiment:

> Nothing on this page is consciously fashioned. While I worked on it, the memory (of the experience under psilocybin) was again reality, and led me at every stroke. For that reason the picture is as many-layered as this memory, and the figure at the lower right is really the captive of its dream. . . . When books about Mexican art came into my hands three weeks later, I again found the motifs of my visions there with a sudden start. . . .

I have also mentioned the occurrence of Mexican motifs in psilocybin inebriation during my first self-experiment with dried *Psilocybe mexicana* mushrooms, as was described in the section on the chemical investigation of these mushrooms. The same phenomenon has also struck R. Gordon Wasson. Proceeding from such observations, he has advanced the conjecture that ancient Mexican art could have been influenced by visionary images, as they appear in mushroom inebriation.

The "Magic Morning Glory" Ololiuhqui

After we had managed to solve the riddle of the sacred mushroom *teonanácatl* in a relatively short time, I also became interested in the problem of another Mexican magic drug not yet chemically elucidated, *ololiuhqui*. *Ololiuhqui* is the Aztec name for the seeds of certain climbing plants (*Convolvulaceae*) that, like the mescaline cactus *péyotl* and the *teonanácatl* mushrooms, were used in pre-Columbian times by the Aztecs and neighboring people in religious ceremonies and magical healing practices. *Ololiuhqui* is still used even today by certain Indian tribes like the Zapotec, Chinantec, Mazatec, and Mixtec, who until a short time ago still led a geniunely isolated existence, little influenced by Christianity, in the remote mountains of southern Mexico.

An excellent study of the historical, ethnological, and botanical aspects of *ololiuhqui* was published in 1941 by Richard Evans Schultes, director of the Harvard Botanical Museum in Cambridge, Massachusetts. It is entitled "A Contribution to Our Knowledge of *Rivea corymbosa*, the Narcotic *Ololiuqui* of the Aztecs." The following statements about the history of *ololiuhqui* derive chiefly from Schultes's monograph.*

The earliest records about this drug were written by Spanish chroniclers of the sixteenth century, who also mentioned *péyotl* and *teonanácatl*. Thus the Franciscan friar Bernardino de Sahagún, in his already cited famous chronicle *Historia General de las Cosas de Nueva España*, writes about the wondrous effects of *ololiuhqui:* "There is an herb, called *coatl xoxouhqui* (green snake), which produces seeds that are called *ololiuhqui*. These seeds stupefy and deprive one of reason: they are taken as a potion."

We obtain further information about these seeds from the physician Francisco Hernández, whom Philip II sent to Mexico from Spain, from 1570 to 1575,

*Translator's note: As R. Gordon Wasson has pointed out, "ololiuhqui" is a more precise orthography than the more popular spelling used by Schultes. See *Botanical Museum Leaflets Harvard University* 20: 161–212, 1963.

in order to study the medicaments of the natives. In the chapter "On Ololiuhqui" of his monumental work entitled *Rerum Medicarum Novae Hispaniae Thesaurus seu Plantarum, Animalium Mineralium Mexicanorum Historia*, published in Rome in 1651, he gives a detailed description and the first illustration of *ololiuhqui*. An extract from the Latin text accompanying the illustration reads in translation: *"Ololiuhqui*, which others call *coaxihuitl* or snake plant, is a climber with thin, green, heart-shaped leaves. . . . The flowers are white, fairly large. . . . The seeds are roundish. . . . When the priests of the Indians wanted to visit with the gods and obtain information from them, they ate of this plant in order to become inebriated. Thousands of fantastic images and demons then appeared to them. . . ." Despite this comparatively good description, the botanical identification of *ololiuhqui* as seeds of *Rivea corymbosa* (L.) Hall. f. occasioned many discussions in specialist circles. Recently preference has been given to the synonym *Turbina corymbosa* (L.) Raf.

When I decided in 1959 to attempt the isolation of the active principles of *ololiuhqui*, only a single report on chemical work with the seeds of *Turbina corymbosa* was available. It was the work of the pharmacologist C. G. Santesson of Stockholm, from the year 1937. Santesson, however, was not successful in isolating an active substance in pure form.

Contradictory findings had been published about the activity of the *ololiuhqui* seeds. The psychiatrist H. Osmond conducted a self-experiment with the seeds of *Turbina corymbosa* in 1955. After the ingestion of 60 to 100 seeds, he entered into a state of apathy and emptiness, accompanied by enhanced visual sensitivity. After four hours, there followed a period of relaxation and well-being, lasting for a longer time. The results of

V. J. Kinross-Wright, published in England in 1958, in which eight voluntary research subjects, who had taken up to 125 seeds, perceived no effects at all, contradicted this report.

Through the mediation of R. Gordon Wasson, I obtained two samples of *ololiuhqui* seeds. In his accompanying letter of 6 August 1959 from Mexico City, he wrote of them:

> . . . The parcels that I am sending you are the following: . . .
>
> A small parcel of seeds that I take to be *Rivea corymbosa*, otherwise known as *ololiuqui*, well-known narcotic of the Aztecs, called in Huautla "la semilla de la Virgen." This parcel, you will find, consists of two little bottles, which represent two deliveries of seeds made to us in Huautla, and a larger batch of seeds, delivered to us by Francisco Ortega "Chico," the Zapotec guide, who himself gathered the seeds from the plants at the Zapotec town of San Bartolo Yautepec. . . .

The first-named, round, light brown seeds from Huautla proved in the botanical determination to have been correctly identified as *Rivea (Turbina) corymbosa*, while the black, angular seeds from San Bartolo Yautepec were identified as *Ipomoea violacea* L.

While *Turbina corymbosa* thrives only in tropical or subtropical climates, one also finds *Ipomoea violacea* as an ornamental plant dispersed over the whole earth in the temperate zones. It is the morning glory that delights the eye in our gardens, in diverse varieties with blue or blue-red striped calyxes.

The Zapotec, besides the original *ololiuhqui* (that is,

the seeds of *Turbina corymbosa,* which they call *badoh*), also utilize *badoh negro,* the seeds of *Ipomoea violacea.* T. MacDougall, who furnished us with a second larger consignment of the last-named seeds, made this observation.

My capable laboratory assistant Hans Tscherter, with whom I had already carried out the isolation of the active principles of the mushrooms, participated in the chemical investigation of the *ololiuhqui* drug. We advanced the working hypothesis that the active principles of the *ololiuhqui* seeds could be representatives of the same class of chemical substances, the indole compounds, to which LSD, psilocybin, and psilocin belong. Considering the very great number of other groups of substances that, like the indoles, were under consideration as active principles of *ololiuhqui,* it was indeed extremely improbable that this assumption would prove true. It could, however, very easily be tested. The presence of indole compounds, of course, may simply and rapidly be determined by colorimetric reactions. Thus even traces of indole substances, with a certain reagent, give an intense blue-colored solution.

We had luck with our hypothesis. Extracts of *ololiuhqui* seeds with the appropriate reagent gave the blue coloration characteristic of indole compounds. With the help of this colorimetric test, we succeeded in a short time in isolating the indole substances from the seeds and in obtaining them in chemically pure form. Their identification led to an astonishing result. What we found appeared at first scarcely believable. Only after repetition and the most careful scrutiny of the operations was our suspicion concerning the peculiar findings eliminated: the active principles from the ancient Mexican magic drug *ololiuhqui* proved to be identical with substances that were already present in my laboratory. They were identical with alkaloids that had been obtained in the course of the decades-long investigations of ergot; partly isolated as such from ergot, partly obtained through chemical modification of ergot substances.

Lysergic acid amide, lysergic acid hydroxyethylamide, and alkaloids closely related to them chemically were established as the main active principles of *ololiuhqui*. (See formulae in the appendix.) Also present was the alkaloid ergobasine, whose synthesis had constituted the starting point of my investigations on ergot alkaloids. Lysergic acid amide and lysergic acid hydroxyethylamide, active principles of *ololiuhqui*, are chemically very closely related to lysergic acid diethylamide (LSD), which even for the nonchemist follows from the names.

Lysergic acid amide was described for the first time by the English chemists S. Smith and G. M. Timmis as a cleavage product of ergot alkaloids, and I had also produced this substance synthetically in the course of the investigations in which LSD originated. Certainly, nobody at the time could have suspected that this compound synthesized in the flask would be discovered twenty years later as a naturally occurring active principle of an ancient Mexican magic drug.

After the discovery of the psychic effects of LSD, I had also tested lysergic acid amide in a self-experiment and established that it likewise evoked a dreamlike condition, but only with about a tenfold to twentyfold greater dose than LSD. This effect was characterized by a sensation of mental emptiness and the unreality and meaninglessness of the outer world, by enhanced sensitivity of hearing, and by a not unpleasant physical lassitude, which ultimately led to sleep. This picture of the effects of LA-111, as lysergic acid amide was called as a research preparation, was confirmed in a systematic investigation by the psychiatrist Dr. H. Solms.

When I presented the findings of our investigations on *ololiuhqui* at the Natural Products Congress of the International Union for Pure and Applied Chemistry (IUPAC) in Sydney, Australia, in the fall of 1960, my colleagues received my talk with skepticism. In the discussions following my lecture, some persons voiced the suspicion that the *ololiuhqui* extracts could well have been contaminated with traces of lysergic acid derivatives, with which so much work had been done in my laboratory.

There was another reason for the doubt in specialist circles concerning our findings. The occurrence in higher plants (i.e., in the morning glory family) of ergot alkaloids that hitherto had been known only as constituents of lower fungi, contradicted the experience that certain substances are typical of and restricted to respective plant families. It is indeed a very rare exception to find a characteristic group of substances, in this case the ergot alkaloids, occurring in two divisions of the plant kingdom broadly separated in evolutionary history.

Our results were confirmed, however, when different laboratories in the United States, Germany, and Holland subsequently verified our investigations on the *ololiuhqui* seeds. Nevertheless, the skepticism went so far that some persons even considered the possibility that the seeds could have been infected with alkaloid-producing fungi. That suspicion, however, was ruled out experimentally.

These studies on the active principles of *ololiuhqui* seeds, although they were published only in professional journals, had an unexpected sequel. We were apprised by two Dutch wholesale seed companies that their sale of seeds of *Ipomoea violacea*, the ornamental blue morning glory, had reached unusual proportions in recent times. They had heard that the great demand was connected with investigations of these seeds in our laboratory, about which they were eager to learn the details. It turned out that the new demand derived from hippie circles and other groups interested in hallucinogenic drugs. They believed they had found in the *ololiuhqui* seeds a substitute for LSD, which was becoming less and less accessible.

The morning glory seed boom, however, lasted only a comparatively short time, evidently because of the undesirable experiences that those in the drug world had with this "new" ancient inebriant. The *ololiuhqui* seeds, which are taken crushed with water or another mild beverage, taste very bad and are difficult for the stomach to digest. Moreover, the psychic effects of *ololiuhqui*, in fact, differ from those of LSD in that the euphoric and the hallucinogenic components are less pronounced, while a sensation of mental emptiness, often anxiety and depression, predominates. Furthermore, weariness and lassitude are hardly desirable effects as traits in an inebriant. These could all be reasons why the drug culture's interest in the morning glory seeds has diminished.

Only a few investigations have considered the question whether the active principles of *ololiuhqui* could find a useful application in medicine. In my opinion, it would be worthwhile to clarify above all whether the strong narcotic, sedative effect of certain *ololiuhqui* constituents, or of chemical modifications of these, is medicinally useful.

My studies in the field of hallucinogenic drugs reached a kind of logical conclusion with the investigations of *ololiuhqui*. They now formed a circle, one could almost say a magic circle: the starting point had been the synthesis of lysergic acid amides, among them the naturally occurring ergot alkaloid ergobasin. This led to the synthesis of lysergic acid diethylamide, LSD. The hallucinogenic properties of LSD were the reason why the hallucinogenic magic mushroom *teonanácatl* found its way into my laboratory. The work with *teonanácatl*, from which psilocybin and psilocin were isolated, proceeded to the investigation of another Mexican magic drug, *ololiuhqui*, in which hallucinogenic principles in the form of lysergic acid amides were again encountered, including ergobasin—with which the magic circle closed.

In Search of the Magic Plant "Ska Maria Pastora" in the Mazatec Country

R. Gordon Wasson, with whom I had maintained friendly relations since the investigations of the Mexican magic mushrooms, invited my wife and me to take part in an expedition to Mexico in the fall of 1962. The purpose of the journey was to search for another Mexican magic plant. Wasson had learned on his travels in the mountains of southern Mexico that the expressed juice of the leaves of a plant, which were called *hojas de la Pastora* or *hojas de María Pastora*, in Mazatec *ska Pastora* or ska *María Pastora* (leaves of the shepherdess or leaves of Mary the shepherdess), were used among the Mazatec in medico-religious practices, like the *teonanácatl* mushrooms and the *ololiuhqui* seeds.

The question now was to ascertain from what sort of plant the "leaves of Mary the shepherdess" derived, and then to identify this plant botanically. We also hoped, if at all possible, to gather sufficient plant material to conduct a chemical investigation on the hallucinogenic principles it contained.

Ride through the Sierra Mazateca

On 26 September 1962, my wife and I accordingly flew to Mexico City, where we met Gordon Wasson. He had made all the necessary preparations for the expedition, so that in two days we had already set out on the next leg of the journey to the south. Mrs. Irmgard Weitlaner Johnson, (widow of Jean B. Johnson, a pioneer of the ethnographic study of the Mexican magic mushrooms, killed in the Allied landing in North Africa) had joined us. Her father, Robert J. Weitlaner, had emigrated to Mexico from Austria and had likewise contributed toward the rediscovery of the mushroom cult. Mrs. Johnson worked at the National Museum of Anthropology in Mexico City, as an expert on Indian textiles.

After a two-day journey in a spacious Land Rover, which took us over the plateau, along the snow-capped Popocatépetl, passing Puebla, down into the Valley of Orizaba with its magnificent tropical vegetation, then by ferry across the Popoloápan (Butterfly River), on through the former Aztec garrison Tuxtepec, we arrived at the starting point of our expedition, the Mazatec village of Jalapa de Díaz, lying on a hillside.

There we were in the midst of the environment and among the people that we would come to know in the succeeding 2½ weeks.

There was an uproar upon our arrival in the marketplace, center of this village widely dispersed in the jungle. Old and young men, who had been squatting and standing around in the half-opened bars and shops, pressed suspiciously yet curiously about our Land Rover; they were mostly barefoot but all wore a *sombrero*. Women and girls were nowhere to be seen. One of the men gave us to understand that we should follow him. He led us to the local president, a fat *mestizo* who had his office in a one-story house with a corrugated iron roof. Gordon showed him our credentials from the civil authorities and from the military governor of Oaxaca, which explained that we had come here to carry out scientific investigations. The president, who probably could not read at all, was visibly impressed by the large-sized documents equipped with official seals. He had lodgings assigned to us in a spacious shed, in which we could place our air mattresses and sleeping bags.

I looked around the region somewhat. The ruins of a large church from colonial times, which must have once been very beautiful, rose almost ghostlike in the direction of an ascending slope at the side of the village square. Now I could also see women looking out of their huts, venturing to examine the strangers. In their long, white dresses, adorned with red borders, and with their long braids of blue-black hair, they offered a picturesque sight.

We were fed by an old Mazatec woman, who directed a young cook and two helpers. She lived in one of the typical Mazatec huts. These are simply rectangular structures with thatched gabled roofs and walls of wooden poles joined together, windowless, the chinks between the wooden poles offering sufficient opportunity to look out. In the middle of the hut, on the stamped clay floor, was an elevated, open fireplace, built up out of dried clay or made of stones. The smoke escaped through large openings in the walls under the two ends of the roof. Bast mats that lay in a corner or along the walls served as beds. The huts were shared with the domestic animals, as well as black swine, turkeys, and chickens. There was roasted chicken to eat, black beans, and also, in place of bread, *tortillas*, a type of cornmeal pancake that is baked on the hot stone slab of the hearth. Beer and tequila, an *Agave* liquor, were served.

Next morning our troop formed for the ride through the Sierra Mazateca. Mules and guides were engaged from the horsekeeper of the village. Guadelupe, the Mazatec familiar with the route, took charge of guiding the lead animal. Gordon, Irmgard, my wife, and I were stationed on our mules in the middle. Teodosio and Pedro, called Chico, two young fellows who trotted along barefoot beside the two mules laden with our baggage, brought up the rear.

It took some time to get accustomed to the hard wooden saddles. Then, however, this mode of locomotion proved to be the most ideal type of travel that I know of. The mules followed the leader, single file, at a steady pace. They required no direction at all by the rider. With surprising dexterity, they sought out the best spots along the almost impassable, partly rocky, partly marshy paths, which led through thickets and streams or onto precipitous slopes. Relieved of all travel cares, we could devote all our attention to the beauty of the landscape and the tropical vegetation. There were tropical forests with gigantic trees overgrown with twining plants, then again clearings with banana groves or coffee plantations, between light stands of trees, flowers at the edge of the path, over which wondrous butterflies bustled about. . . . We made our way upstream along the broad riverbed of Rio Santo Domingo, with brooding heat and steamy air, now steeply ascending, then again falling. During a short, violent tropical downpour, the long broad ponchos of oilcloth, with which Gordon had equipped us, proved quite useful. Our Indian guides had protected themselves from the cloudburst with gigantic, heart-shaped leaves that they nimbly chopped off at the edge of the path. Teodosio and Chico gave the impression of great, green hay ricks as they ran, covered with these leaves, beside their mules.

Shortly before nightfall we arrived at the first settlement, La Providencia ranch. The patron, Don Joaquin García, the head of a large family, welcomed us hospitably and full of dignity. It was impossible to determine how many children, in addition to the grown-ups and the domestic animals, were present in the large living room, feebly illuminated by the hearth fire alone.

Gordon and I placed our sleeping bags outdoors under the projecting roof. I awoke in the morning to find a pig grunting over my face.

After another day's journey on the backs of our worthy mules, we arrived at Ayautla, a Mazatec settlement spread across a hillside. En route, among the shrubbery, I had delighted in the blue calyxes of the magic morning glory *Ipomoea violacea,* the mother plant of the *ololiuhqui* seeds. It grew wild there, whereas among us it is only found in the Garden as an ornamental plant.

We remained in Ayautla for several days. We had lodging in the house of Doña Donata Sosa de García. Doña Donata was in charge of a large family, which included her ailing husband. In addition, she presided over the coffee cultivation of the region. The collection center for the freshly picked coffee beans was in an adjacent building. It was a lovely picture, the young Indian woman and girls returning home from the harvest toward evening, in their bright garments adorned with colored borders, the coffee sacks carried on their backs by headbands. Doña Donata also managed a type of grocery store, in which her husband, Don Eduardo, stood behind the counter.

In the evening by candlelight, Doña Donata, who

besides Mazatec also spoke Spanish, told us about life in the village; one tragedy or another had already struck nearly every one of the seemingly peaceful huts that lay surrounded by this paradisiacal scenery. A man who had murdered his wife, and who now sits in prison for life, had lived in the house next door, which now stood empty. The husband of a daughter of Doña Donata, after an affair with another woman, was murdered out of jealousy. The president of Ayautla, a young bull of a *mestizo*, to whom we had made our formal visit in the afternoon, never made the short walk from his hut to his "office" in the village hall (with the corrugated iron roof) unless accompanied by two heavily armed men. Because he exacted illegal taxes, he was afraid of being shot to death. Since no higher authority sees to justice in this remote region, people have recourse to self-defense of this type.

Thanks to Doña Donata's good connections, we received the first sample of the sought-after plant, some leaves of *hojas de la Pastora*, from an old woman. Since the flowers and roots were missing, however, this plant material was not suitable for botanical identification. Our efforts to obtain more precise information about the habitat of the plant and its use were also fruitless.

The continuation of our journey from Ayautla was delayed, as we had to wait until our boys could again bring back the mules that they had taken to pasture on the other side of Rio Santo Domingo, over the river swollen by intense downpours.

After a two-day ride, on which we had passed the night in the high mountain village of San Miguel-Huautla, we arrived at Rio Santiago. Here we were joined by Doña Herlinda Martinez Cid, a teacher from Huautla de Jiménez. She had ridden over on the invitation of Gordon Wasson, who had known her since his mushroom expeditions, and was to serve as our Mazatec and Spanish-speaking interpreter. Moreover, she could help us, through her numerous relatives scattered in the region, to pave the way to contacts with *curanderos* and *curanderas* who used the *hojas de la Pastora* in their practice. Because of our delayed arrival in Rio Santiago, Doña Herlinda, who was acquainted with the dangers of the region, had been apprehensive about us, fearing we might have plunged down a rocky path or been attacked by robbers.

Our next stop was in San José Tenango, a settlement lying deep in a valley, in the midst of tropical vegetation with orange and lemon trees and banana plantations. Here again was the typical village picture: in the center, a marketplace with a half-ruined church from the colonial period, with two or three stands, a general store, and shelters for horses and mules. We found lodging in a corrugated iron barracks, with the special luxury of a cement floor, on which we could spread out our sleeping bags.

In the thick jungle on the mountainside we discovered a spring, whose magnificent fresh water in a natural rocky basin invited us to bathe. That was an unforgettable pleasure after days without opportunities to wash properly. In this grotto I saw a hummingbird for the first time in nature, a blue-green, metallic, iridescent gem, which whirred over great liana blossoms.

The desired contact with persons skilled in medicine came about thanks to the kindred connections of Doña Herlinda, beginning with the *curandero* Don Sabino. But he refused, for some reason, to receive us in a consultation and to question the leaves. From an old *curandera*, a venerable woman in a strikingly magnificent Mazatec garment, with the lovely name Natividad Rosa, we received a whole bundle of flowering specimens of the sought-after plant, but even she could not be prevailed upon to perform a ceremony with the leaves for us. Her excuse was that she was too old for the hardship of the magical trip; she could never cover the long distance to certain places: a spring where the wise women gather their powers, a lake on which the sparrows sing, and where objects get their names. Nor would Natividad Rosa tell us where she had gathered the leaves. They grew in a very, very distant forest valley. Wherever she dug up a plant, she put a coffee bean in the earth as thanks to the gods.

We now possessed ample plants with flowers and roots, which were suitable for botanical identification. It was apparently a representative of the genus *Salvia*, a relative of the well-known meadow sage. The plants had blue flowers crowned with a white dome, which are arranged on a panicle 20 to 30 cm long, whose stem leaked blue.

Several days later, Natividad Rosa brought us a whole basket of leaves, for which she was paid fifty pesos. The business seemed to have been discussed, for two other women brought us further quantities of leaves. As it was known that the expressed juice of the leaves is drunk in the ceremony, and this must therefore contain the active principle, the fresh leaves were crushed on a stone plate, squeezed out in a cloth, the juice diluted with alcohol as a preservative, and decanted into flasks in order to be studied later in the laboratory in Basel. I was assisted in this work by an Indian girl, who was accustomed to dealing with the stone plate, the *metate*, on which the Indians since ancient times have ground their corn by hand.

On the day before the journey was to continue, having given up all hope of being able to attend a ceremony, we suddenly made another contact with a *cu-*

randera, one who was ready "to serve us." A confidante of Herlinda's, who had produced this contact, led us after nightfall along a secret path to the hut of the *curandera,* lying solitary on the mountainside above the settlement. No one from the village was to see us or discover that we were received there. It was obviously considered a betrayal of sacred customs, worthy of punishment, to allow strangers, whites, to take part in this. That indeed had also been the real reason why the other healers whom we asked had refused to admit us to a leaf ceremony. Strange birdcalls from the darkness accompanied us on the ascent, and the barking of dogs was heard on all sides. The dogs had detected the strangers. The *curandera* Consuela García, a woman of some forty years, barefoot like all Indian women in this region, timidly admitted us to her hut and immediately closed up the doorway with a heavy bar. She bid us lie down on the bast mats on the stamped mud floor. As Consuela spoke only Mazatec, Herlinda translated her instructions into Spanish for us. The *curandera* lit a candle on a table covered with some images of saints, along with a variety of rubbish. Then she began to bustle about busily, but in silence. All at once we heard peculiar noises and a rummaging in the room—did the hut harbor some hidden person whose shape and proportions could not be made out in the candlelight? Visibly disturbed, Consuela searched the room with the burning candle. It appeared to be merely rats, however, who were working their mischief. In a bowl the *curandera* now kindled *copal,* an incense-like resin, which soon filled the whole hut with its aroma. Then the magic potion was ceremoniously prepared. Consuela inquired which of us wished to drink of it with her. Gordon announced himself. Since I was suffering from a severe stomach upset at the time, I could not join in. My wife substituted for me.

The *curandera* laid out six pairs of leaves for herself. She apportioned the same number to Gordon. Anita received three pairs. Like the mushrooms, the leaves are always dosed in pairs, a practice that, of course, has a magical significance. The leaves were crushed with the *metate*, then squeezed out through a fine sieve into a cup, and the *metate* and the contents of the sieve were rinsed with water. Finally, the filled cups were incensed over the *copal* vessel with much ceremony. Consuela asked Anita and Gordon, before she handed them their cups, whether they believed in the truth and the holiness of the ceremony. After they answered in the affirmative and the very bitter-tasting potion was solemnly imbibed, the candles were extinguished and, lying in darkness on the bast masts, we awaited the effects.

After some twenty minutes Anita whispered to me that she saw striking, brightly bordered images. Gordon also perceived the effect of the drug. The voice of the *curandera* sounded from the darkness, half speaking, half singing. Herlinda translated: Did we believe in Christ's blood and the holiness of the rites? After our "creemos" ("We believe"), the ceremonial performance continued. The *curandera* lit the candles, moved them from the "altar table" onto the floor, sang and spoke prayers or magic formulas, placed the candles again under the images of the saints—then again silence and darkness. Thereupon the true consultation began. Consuela asked for our request. Gordon inquired after the health of his daughter, who immediately before his departure from New York had to be admitted prematurely to the hospital in expectation of a baby. He received the comforting information that mother and child were well. Then again came singing and prayer and manipulations with the candles on the "altar table" and on the floor, over the smoking basin.

When the ceremony was at an end, the *curandera* asked us to rest yet a while longer in prayer on our bast mats. Suddenly a thunderstorm burst out. Through the cracks of the beam walls, lightning flashed into the darkness of the hut, accompanied by violent thunderbolts, while a tropical downpour raged, beating on the roof. Consuela voiced apprehension that we would not be able to leave her house unseen in the darkness. But the thunderstorm let up before daybreak, and we went down the mountainside to our corrugated iron barracks, as noiselessly as possible by the light of flashlights, unnoticed by the villagers, but dogs again barked from all sides.

Participation in this ceremony was the climax of our expedition. It brought confirmation that the *hojas de la Pastora* were used by the Indians for the same purpose and in the same ceremonial milieu as *teonanácatl*, the sacred mushrooms. Now we also had authentic plant material, not only sufficient for botanical identification, but also for the planned chemical analysis. The inebriated state that Gordon Wasson and my wife had experienced with the *hojas* had been shallow and only of short duration, yet it had exhibited a distinctly hallucinogenic character.

On the morning after this eventful night we took leave of San José Tenango. The guide, Guadelupe, and the two fellows Teodosio and Pedro appeared before our barracks with the mules at the appointed time. Soon packed up and mounted, our little troop then moved uphill again, through the fertile landscape glittering in the sunlight from the night's thunderstorm. Returning by way of Santiago, toward evening we reached our last stop in Mazatec country, the capital Huautla de Jiménez.

From here on, the return trip to Mexico City was made by automobile. With a final supper in the Posada Rosaura, at the time the only inn in Huautla, we took leave of our Indian guides and of the worthy mules that had carried us so surefootedly and in such a pleasant way through the Sierra Mazatec. The Indians were paid off, and Teodosio, who also accepted payment for his chief in Jalapa de Díaz (where the animals were to be returned afterward), gave a receipt with his thumbprint colored by a ballpoint pen. We took up quarters in Doña Herlinda's house.

A day later we made our formal visit to the *curandera* María Sabina, a woman made famous by the Wassons' publications. It had been in her hut that Gordon Wasson became the first white man to taste of the sacred mushrooms, in the course of a nocturnal ceremony in the summer of 1955. Gordon and María Sabina greeted each other cordially, as old friends. The *curandera* lived out of the way, on the mountainside above Huautla. The house in which the historic session with Gordon Wasson had taken place had been burned, presumably by angered residents or an envious colleague, because she had divulged the secret of *teonanácatl* to strangers. In the new hut in which we found ourselves, an incredible disorder prevailed, as had probably also prevailed in the old hut, in which half-naked children, hens, and pigs bustled about. The old *curandera* had an intelligent face, exceptionally changeable in expression. She was obviously impressed when it was explained that we had managed to confine the spirit of the mushrooms in pills, and she at once declared herself ready to "serve us" with these, that is, to grant us a consultation. It was agreed that this should take place the coming night in the house of Doña Herlinda.

In the course of the day I took a stroll through Huautla de Jiménez, which led along a main street on the mountainside. Then I accompanied Gordon on his visit to the Instituto Nacional Indigenista. This governmental organization had the duty of studying and helping to solve the problems of the indigenous population, that is, the Indians. Its leader told us of the difficulties that the "coffee policy" had caused in the area at that time. The president of Huautla, in collaboration with the Instituto Nacional Indigenista had tried to eliminate middlemen in order to shape the coffee prices favorably for the producing Indians. His body was found, mutilated, the previous June.

Our stroll also took us past the cathedral, from which Gregorian chants resounded. Old Father Aragon, whom Gordon knew well from his earlier stays, invited us into the vestry for a glass of tequila.

A Mushroom Ceremony

As we returned home to Herlinda's house toward evening, María Sabina had already arrived there with a large company, her two lovely daughters, Apolonia and Aurora (two prospective *curanderas*), and a niece, all of whom brought children along with them. Whenever her child began to cry, Apolonia would offer her breast to it. The old *curandero* Don Aurelio also appeared, a mighty man, one-eyed, in a black-and-white patterned *serape* (cloak). Cacao and sweet pastry were served on the veranda. I was reminded of the report from an ancient chronicle which described how *chocolatl* was drunk before the ingestion of *teonanácatl*.

After the fall of darkness, we all proceeded into the room in which the ceremony would take place. It was then locked up—that is, the door was obstructed with the only bed available. Only an emergency exit into the back garden remained unlatched for absolute necessity. It was nearly midnight when the ceremony began. Until that time the whole party lay, in darkness sleeping or awaiting the night's events, on the bast mats spread on the floor. María Sabina threw a piece of *copal* on the embers of a brazier from time to time, whereby the stuffy air in the crowded room became somewhat bearable. I had explained to the *curandera* through Herlinda, who was again with the party as interpreter, that one pill contained the spirit of two pairs of mushrooms. (The pills contained 5.0 mg synthetic psilocybin apiece.)

When all was ready, María Sabina apportioned the pills in pairs among the grown-ups present. After solemn smoking, she herself took two pairs (corresponding to 20 mg psilocybin). She gave the same dose to Don Aurelio and her daughter Apolonia, who would also serve as *curandera*. Aurora received one pair, as did Gordon, while my wife and Irmgard got only one pill each.

One of the children, a girl of about ten, under the guidance of María Sabina, had prepared for me the juice of five pairs of fresh leaves of *hojas de la Pastora*. I wanted to experience this drug that I had been unable to try in San José Tenango. The potion was said to be especially active when prepared by an innocent child. The cup with the expressed juice was likewise incensed and conjured by María Sabina and Don Aurelio, before it was delivered to me.

All of these preparations and the following ceremony progressed in much the same way as the consultation with the *curandera* Consuela García in San José Tenango.

After the drug was apportioned and the candle on the "altar" was extinguished, we awaited the effects in the darkness.

Before a half hour had elapsed, the *curandera* murmured something; her daughter and Don Aurelio also became restless. Herlinda translated and explained to us what was wrong. María Sabina had said that the pills lacked the spirit of the mushrooms. I discussed the situation with Gordon, who lay beside me. For us it was clear that absorption of the active principle from the pills, which must first dissolve in the stomach, occurs more slowly than from the mushrooms, in which some of the active principle already becomes absorbed through the mucous membranes during chewing. But how could we give a scientific explanation under such conditions? Rather than try to explain, we decided to act. We distributed more pills. Both *curanderas* and the *curandero* each received another pair. They had now each taken a total dosage of 30 mg psilocybin.

After about another quarter of an hour, the spirit of the pills did begin to yield its effects, which lasted until the crack of dawn. The daughters, and Don Aurelio with his deep bass voice, fervently answered the prayers and singing of the *curandera*. Blissful, yearning moans of Apolonia and Aurora, between singing and prayer, gave the impression that the religious experience of the young women in the drug inebriation was combined with sensual-sexual feelings.

In the middle of the ceremony María Sabina asked for our request. Gordon inquired again after the health of his daughter and grandchild. He received the same good information as from the *curandera* Consuela. Mother and child were in fact well when he returned home to New York. Obviously, however, this still represents no proof of the prophetic abilities of both *curanderas*.

Evidently as an effect of the *hojas*, I found myself for some time in a state of mental sensitivity and intense experience, which, however, was not accompanied by hallucinations. Anita, Irmgard, and Gordon experienced a euphoric condition of inebriation that was influenced by the strange, mystical atmosphere. My wife was impressed by the vision of very distinct strange line patterns.

She was astonished and perplexed, later, on discovering precisely the same images in the rich ornamentation over the altar in an old church near Puebla. That was on the return trip to Mexico City, when we visited churches from colonial times. These admirable churches offer great cultural and historical interest because the Indian artists and workmen who assisted in their construction smuggled in elements of Indian style. Klaus Thomas, in his book *Die künstlich gesteuerte Seele* [The artificially steered mind] (Ferdinand Enke Verlag, Stuttgart, 1970), writes about the possible influence of visions from psilocybin inebriation on Meso-American Indian art: "Surely a cultural-historical comparison of the old and new creations of Indian art . . . must convince the unbiased spectator of the harmony with the images, forms and colors of a psilocybin inebriation." The Mexican character of the visions seen in my first experience with dried *Psilocybe mexicana* mushrooms and the drawing of Li Gelpke after a psilocybin inebriation could also point to such an association.

As we took leave of María Sabina and her clan at the crack of dawn, the *curandera* said that the pills had the same power as the mushrooms, that there was no difference. This was a confirmation from the most competent authority, that the synthetic psilocybin is identical with the natural product. As a parting gift I let María Sabina have a vial of psilocybin pills. She radiantly explained to our interpreter Herlinda that she could now give consultations even in the season when no mushrooms grow.

How should we judge the conduct of María Sabina,

the fact that she allowed strangers, white people, access to the secret ceremony, and let them try the sacred mushroom?

To her credit it can be said that she had thereby opened the door to the exploration of the Mexican mushroom cult in its present form, and to the scientific, botanical, and chemical investigation of the sacred mushrooms. Valuable active substances, psilocybin and psilocin, resulted. Without this assistance, the ancient knowledge and experience that was concealed in these secret practices would possibly, even probably, have disappeared without a trace, without having borne fruit, in the advancement of Western civilization.

From another standpoint, the conduct of this *curandera* can be regarded as a profanation of a sacred custom—even as a betrayal. Some of her countrymen were of this opinion, which was expressed in acts of revenge, including the burning of her house.

The profanation of the mushroom cult did not stop with the scientific investigations. The publication about the magic mushrooms unleashed an invasion of hippies and drug seekers into the Mazatec country, many of whom behaved badly, some even criminally. Another undesirable consequence was the beginning of true tourism in Huautla de Jiménez, whereby the originality of the place was eradicated.

Such statements and considerations are, for the most part, the concern of ethnographical research. Wherever researchers and scientists trace and elucidate the remains of ancient customs that are becoming rarer, their primitiveness is lost. This loss is only more or less counterbalanced when the outcome of the research represents a lasting cultural gain.

From Huautla de Jiménez we proceeded first to Teotitlán, in a breakneck truck ride along a half-paved road, and from there went on a comfortable car trip back to Mexico City, the starting point of our expedition. I had lost several kilograms in body weight, but was overwhelmingly compensated in enchanting experiences.

The herbarium samples of *hojas de la Pastora*, which we had brought with us, were subjected to botanical indentification by Carl Epling and Carlos D. Játiva at the Botanical Institute of Harvard University in Cambridge, Massachusetts. They found that this plant was a hitherto undescribed species of *Salvia*, which was named *Salvia divinorum* by these authors.

The chemical investigation of the juice of the magic sage in the laboratory in Basel was unsuccessful. The psychoactive principle of this drug seems to be a rather unstable substance, since the juice prepared in Mexico and preserved with alcohol proved in self-experiments to be no longer active.

Where the chemical nature of the active principle is concerned, the problem of the magic plant *ska María Pastora* still awaits solution.

So far in this book I have mainly described my scientific work and matters relating to my professional activity. But this work, by its very nature, had repercussions on my own life and personality, not least because it brought me into contact with interesting and important contemporaries. I have already mentioned some of them—Timothy Leary, Rudolf Gelpke, Gordon Wasson. Now, in the pages that follow, I would like to emerge from the natural scientist's reserve, in order to portray encounters which were personally meaningful to me and which helped me solve questions posed by the substances I had discovered.

7

Radiance from Ernst Jünger

Radiance is the perfect term to express the influence that Ernst Jünger's literary work and personality have had on me. In the light of his perspective, which stereoscopically comprises the surfaces and depths of things, the world I knew took on a new, translucent splendor. That happened a long time before the discovery of LSD and before I came into personal contact with this author in connection with hallucinogenic drugs.

My enchantment with Ernst Jünger began with his book *Das Abenteuerliche Herz* [The adventurous heart]. Again and again in the last forty years I have taken up this book. Here more than ever, in themes that weigh more lightly and lie closer to me than war and a new type of human being (subjects of Jünger's earlier books), the beauty and magic of Jünger's prose was opened to me—descriptions of flowers, of dreams, of solitary walks; thoughts about chance, the future, colors, and about other themes that have direct relation to our personal lives. Everywhere in his prose the miracle of creation became evident, in the precise description of the surfaces and, in translucence, of the depths; and the uniqueness and the imperishable in every human being was touched upon. No other writer has thus opened my eyes.

Drugs were also mentioned in *Das Abenteuerliche Herz*. Many years passed, however, before I myself began to be especially interested in this subject, after the discovery of the psychic effects of LSD.

My first correspondence with Ernst Jünger had nothing to do with the context of drugs; rather I once wrote to him on his birthday, as a thankful reader.

Bottmingen, 29 March 1947

Dear Mr. Jünger,

As one richly endowed by you for years, I wished to send a jar of honey to you for your birthday. But I did not have this pleasure, because my export license has been refused in Bern.

The gift was intended less as a greeting from a country in which milk and honey still flow, than as a reminiscence of the enchanting sentences in your book *Auf den Marmorklippen* (On the Marble Cliffs), where you speak of the "golden bees."

The book mentioned here had appeared in 1939, just shortly before the outbreak of World War II. *Auf den Marmorklippen* is not only a masterpiece of German prose, but also a work of great significance because in this book the characteristics of tyrants and the horror of war and nocturnal bombardment are described prophetically, in poetic vision.

In the course of our correspondence, Ernst Jünger

also inquired about my LSD studies, of which he had learned through a friend. Thereupon I sent him the pertinent publications, which he acknowledged with the following comments:

Kirchhorst, 3/3/1948

. . . together with both enclosures concerning your new phantasticum. It seems indeed that you have entered a field that contains so many tempting mysteries.

Your consignment came together with the *Confessions of an English Opium Eater*, that has just been published in a new translation. The translator writes me that his reading of *Das Abenteuerliche Herz* stimulated him to do his work.

As far as I am concerned, my practical studies in this field are far behind me. These are experiments in which one sooner or later embarks on truly dangerous paths, and may be considered lucky to escape with only a black eye.

What interested me above all was the relationship of these substances to productivity. It has been my experience, however, that creative achievement requires an alert consciousness, and that it diminishes under the spell of drugs. On the other hand, conceptualization is important, and one gains insights under the influence of drugs that indeed are not possible otherwise. I consider the beautiful essay that Maupassant has written about ether to be such an insight. Moreover, I had the impression that in fever one also discovers new landscapes, new archipelagos, and a new music, that becomes completely distinct when the "customs station"* appears. For geographic description, on the other hand, one must be fully conscious. What productivity means to the artist, healing means to the physician. Accordingly, it also may suffice for him that he sometimes enters the regions through the tapestries that our senses have woven. Moreover, I seem to perceive in our time less of a taste for the phantastica than for the energetica— amphetamine, which has even been furnished to fliers and other soldiers by the armies, belongs to this group. Tea is in my opinion a phantasticum, coffee an energeticum—tea therefore possesses a disproportionately higher artistic rank. I notice that coffee disrupts the delicate lattice of light and shadows, the fruitful doubts that emerge during the writing of a sentence. One exceeds his inhibitions. With tea, on the other hand, the thoughts climb genuinely upward.

So far as my "studies" are concerned, I had a manuscript on that topic, but have since burned it. My excursions terminated with hashish, that led to very pleasant, but also to manic states, to oriental tyranny. . . .

Soon afterward, in a letter from Ernst Jünger I learned that he had inserted a discourse about drugs in the novel *Heliopolis*, on which he was then working. He wrote to me about the drug researcher who figures in the novel:

*"An der Zollstation" [At the custom station], the title heading of a section in *Das Abenteuerliche Herz* (2d ed.) that concerns the transition from life to death.

Among the trips in the geographical and metaphysical worlds, which I am attempting to describe there, are those of a purely sedentary man, who explores the archipelagos beyond the navigable seas, for which he uses drugs as a vehicle. I give extracts from his log book. Certainly, I cannot allow this Columbus of the inner globe to end well—he dies of a poisoning. *Avis au lecteur.*

The book that appeared the following year bore the subtitle *Rückblick auf eine Stadt* [Retrospective on a city], a retrospective on a city of the future, in which technical apparatus and the weapons of the present time were developed still further in magic, and in which power struggles between a demonic technocracy and a conservative force took place. In the figure of Antonio Peri, Jünger depicted the mentioned drug researcher, who resided in the ancient city of Heliopolis.

He captured dreams, just like others appear to chase after butterflies with nets. He did not travel to the islands on Sundays and holidays and did not frequent the taverns on Pagos beach. He locked himself up in his studio for trips into the dreamy regions. He said that all countries and unknown islands were woven into the tapestry. The drugs served him as keys to entry into the chambers and caves of this world. In the course of the years he had gained great knowledge, and he kept a log book of his excursions. A small library adjoined this studio, consisting partly of herbals and medicinal reports, partly of works by poets and magicians. Antonio tended to read there while the effect of the drug itself developed. . . . He went on voyages of discovery in the universe of his brain. . . .

In the center of this library, which was pillaged by mercenaries of the provincial governor during the arrest of Antonio Peri, stood

> The great inspirers of the nineteenth century: De Quincey, E.T.A. Hoffmann, Poe, and Baudelaire. Yet there were also books from the ancient past: herbals, necromancy texts, and demonology of the middle-aged world. They included the names Albertus Magnus, Raimundus Lullus, and Agrippa of Nettesheym. . . . Moreover, there was the great folio *De Praestigiis Daemonum* by Wierus, and the very unique compilations of Medicus Weckerus, published in Basel in 1582. . . .

In another part of his collection, Antonio Peri seemed to have cast his attention principally "on ancient pharmacology books, formularies and pharmacopoeias, and to have hunted for reprints of journals and annals. Among others was found a heavy old volume by the Heidelberg psychologists on the extract of mescal buttons, and a paper on the phantastica of ergot by Hofmann-Bottmingen. . . ."

In the same year in which *Heliopolis* came out, I made the personal acquaintance of the author. I went to meet Ernst Jünger in Ravensburg, for a Swiss sojourn. On a wonderful fall journey in southern Switzerland, together with mutual friends, I experienced the radiant power of his personality.

Two years later, at the beginning of February 1951,

came the great adventure, an LSD trip with Ernst Jünger. Since, up until that moment, there were only reports of LSD experiments in connection with psychiatric inquiries, this experiment especially interested me, because this was an opportunity to observe the effects of LSD on the artistic person, in a nonmedical milieu. That was still somewhat before Aldous Huxley, from the same perspective, began to experiment with mescaline, about which he then reported in his two books *The Doors of Perception* and *Heaven and Hell*.

In order to have medical aid on hand if necessary, I invited my friend, the physician and pharmacologist Professor Heribert Konzett, to participate. The trip took place at 10:00 in the morning, in the living room of our house in Bottmingen. Since the reaction of such a highly sensitive man as Ernst Jünger was not foreseeable, a low dose was chosen for this first experiment as a precaution, only 0.05 mg. The experiment then, did not lead into great depths.

The beginning phase was characterized by the intensification of aesthetic experience. Red-violet roses were of unknown luminosity and radiated in portentous brightness. The concerto for flute and harp by Mozart was perceived in its celestial beauty as heavenly music. In mutual astonishment we contemplated the haze of smoke that ascended with the ease of thought from a Japanese incense stick. As the inebriation became deeper and the conversation ended, we came to fantastic reveries while we lay in our easy chairs with closed eyes. Ernst Jünger enjoyed the color display of oriental images: I was on a trip among Berber tribes in North Africa, saw colored caravans and lush oases. Heribert Konzett, whose features seemed to me to be transfigured, Buddha-like, experienced a breath of timelessness, liberation from the past and the future, blessedness through being completely here and now.

The return from the altered state of consciousness was associated with strong sensitivity to cold. Like freezing travelers, we enveloped ourselves in covers for the landing. The return to everyday reality was celebrated with a good dinner, in which Burgundy flowed copiously.

This trip was characterized by the mutuality and parallelism of our experiences, which were perceived as profoundly joyful. All three of us had drawn near the gate to an experience of mystical being; however, it did not open. The dose we had chosen was too low. In misunderstanding this reason, Ernst Jünger, who had earlier been thrust into deeper realms by a high dose of mescaline, remarked: "Compared with the tiger mescaline, your LSD, is, after all, only a house cat." After later experiments with higher doses of LSD, he revised this estimation.

Jünger has assimilated the mentioned spectacle of the incense stick into literature, in his story *Besuch auf Godenholm* [Visit to Godenholm], in which deeper experiences of drug inebriation also play a part:

Schwarzenberg burned an incense stick, as he sometimes did, to clear the air. A blue plume ascended from the tip of the stick. Moltner looked at it first with astonishment, then with delight, as if a new power of the eyes had come to him. It revealed itself in the play of this fragrant smoke, which ascended from the slender stick and then branched out into a delicate crown. It was as if his imagination had created it—a pallid web of sea lilies in the depths, that scarcely trembled from the beat of the surf. Time was active in this creation—it had circled it, whirled about it, wreathed it, as if imaginary coins rapidly piled up one on top of another. The abundance of space revealed itself in the fiber work, the nerves, which stretched and unfolded in the height, in a vast number of filaments.

Now a breath of air affected the vision, and softly twisted it about the shaft like a dancer. Moltner uttered a shout of surprise. The beams and lattices of the wondrous flower wheeled around in new planes, in new fields. Myriads of molecules observed the harmony. Here the laws no longer acted under the veil of appearance; matter was so delicate and weightless that it clearly reflected them. How simple and cogent everything was. The numbers, masses and weights stood out from matter. They cast off the raiments. No goddess could inform the initiates more boldly and freely. The pyramids with their weight did not reach up to this revelation. That was Pythagorean luster. No spectacle had ever affected him with such a magic spell.

This deepened experience in the aesthetic sphere, as it is described here in the example of contemplation of a haze of blue smoke, is typical of the beginning phase of LSD inebriation, before deeper alterations of conscious begin.

I visited Ernst Jünger occasionally in the following years, in Wilfingen, Germany, where he had moved from Ravensburg; or we met in Switzerland, at my place in Bottmingen, or in Bündnerland in southeastern Switzerland. Through the shared LSD experience our relations had deepened. Drugs and problems connected with them constituted a major subject of our conversation and correspondence, without our having made further practical experiments in the meantime. We exchanged literature about drugs. Ernst Jünger thus let me have for my drug library the rare, valuable monograph of Dr. Ernst Freiherrn von Bibra, *Die Narkotischen Genussmittel und der Mensch* [Narcotic pleasure drugs and man] printed in Nuremburg in 1855. This book is a pioneering, standard work of drug literature, a source of the first order, above all as relates to the history of drugs. What von Bibra embraces under the designation "Narkotischen Genussmittel" are not only substances like opium and thorn apple, but also coffee, tobacco, kat, which do not fall under the present conception of narcotics, any more than do drugs such as coca, fly agaric, and hashish, which he also described.

Noteworthy, and today still as topical as at the time, are the general opinions about drugs that von Bibra contrived more than a century ago:

> The individual who has taken too much hashish, and then runs frantically about in the streets and attacks everyone who confronts him, sinks into insignificance beside the numbers of those who after mealtime pass calm and happy hours with a moderate dose; and the number of those who are able to overcome the heaviest exertions through coca, yes, who were possibly rescued from death by starvation through coca, by far exceed the few *coqueros* who have undermined their health by immoderate use. In the same manner, only a misplaced hypocrisy can condemn the vinous cup of old father Noah, because individual drunkards do not know how to observe limit and moderation.

From time to time I advised Ernst Jünger about actual and entertaining events in the field of inebriating drugs, as in my letter of September 1955:

. . . Last week the first 200 grams of a new drug arrived, whose investigation I wish to take up. It involves the seeds of a mimosa (*Piptadenia peregrina* Benth,) that is used as a stimulating intoxicant by the Indians of the Orinoco. The seeds are ground, fermented, and then mixed with the powder of burned snail shells. This powder is sniffed by the Indians with the help of a hollow, forked bird bone, as already reported by Alexander von Humboldt in *Reise nach den Aequinoctial-Gegenden des Neuen Kontinents* [Voyage to the equinoctial regions of the new continent] (Book 8, Chapter 24). The warlike tribe, the Otomaco, especially use this drug, called *niopo, yupa, nopo* or *cojoba*, to an extensive degree, even today. It is reported in the monograph by P. J. Gumilla, S. J. (*El Orinoco Ilustrado*, 1741): "The Otomacos sniffed the powder before they went to battle with the Caribes, for in earlier times there existed savage wars between these tribes. . . . This drug robs them completely of reason, and they frantically seize their weapons. And if the women were not so adept at holding them back and binding them fast, they would daily cause horrible devastation. It is a terrible vice. . . . Other benign and docile tribes that also sniff the *yupa*, do not get into such a fury as the Otomacos, who through self-injury with this agent made themselves completely cruel before combat, and marched into battle with savage fury."

I am curious how *niopo* would act on people like us. Should a *niopo* session one day come to pass, then we should on no account send our wives away, as on that early spring reverie,* that they may bind us fast if necessary. . . .

Chemical analysis of this drug led to isolation of active principles that, like the ergot alkaloids and psilocybin, belong to the group of indole alkaloids, but which were already described in the technical literature, and were therefore not investigated further in the Sandoz laboratories.** The fantastic effects described above appeared to occur only with the particular manner of use as snuff powder, and also seemed to be related, in all probability, to the psychic structure of the Indian tribes concerned.

Ambivalence of Drug Use

Fundamental questions of drug problems were dealt with in the following correspondence.

Bottmingen, 16 December 1961

Dear Mr. Jünger,
On the one hand, I would have the great desire, besides the natural-scientific, chemical-pharmacological investigation of hallu-cinogenic substances, also to research their use as magic drugs in other regions. . . .
On the other hand, I must admit that the

*The LSD trip of February 1951 is meant here.

**Translator's note: The active principles of *niopo* are DMT (N,N-dimethyltryptamine) and its congeners. DMT was first prepared in 1931 by Manske.

fundamental question very much occupies me, whether the use of these types of drugs, namely of substances that so deeply affect our minds, could not indeed represent a forbidden transgression of limits. As long as any means or methods are used, which provide only an additional, newer aspect of reality, surely there is nothing to object to in such means; on the contrary, the experience and the knowledge of further facets of *the* reality only makes this reality ever more real to us. The question exists, however, whether the deeply affecting drugs under discussion here will in fact only open an additional window for our senses and perceptions, or whether the spectator himself, the core of his being, undergoes alterations. The latter would signify that something is altered that in my opinion should always remain intact. My concern is addressed to the question, whether the innermost core of our being is actually unimpeachable, and cannot become damaged by whatever happens in its material, physical-chemical, biological and psychic shells—or whether matter in the form of these drugs displays a potency that has the ability to attack the spiritual center of the personality, the self. The latter would have to be explained by the fact that the effect of magic drugs happens at the borderline where mind and matter merge—that these magic substances are themselves cracks in the infinite realm of matter, in which the depth of matter, its relationship with the mind, becomes particularly obvious. This could be expressed by a modification of the familiar words of Goethe:

157

"Were the eye not sunny,
It could never behold the sun;
If the power of the mind were not in
    matter,
How could matter disturb the mind."

This would correspond to cracks which the radioactive substances constitute in the periodic system of the elements, where the transition of matter into energy becomes manifest. Indeed, one must ask whether the production of atomic energy likewise represents a transgression of forbidden limits.

A further disquieting thought, which follows from the possibility of influencing the highest intellectual functions by traces of a substance, concerns free will.

The highly active psychotropic substances like LSD and psilocybin possess in their chemical structure a very close relationship with substances inherent in the body, which are found in the central nervous system and play an important role in the regulation of its functions. It is therefore conceivable that through some disturbance in the metabolism of the normal neurotransmitters, a compound like LSD or psilocybin is formed, which can determine and alter the character of the individual, his world view and his behavior. A trace of a substance, whose production or nonproduction we cannot control with our wills, has the power to shape our destiny. Such biochemical considerations could have led to the sentence that Gottfried Benn quoted in his essay "Provoziertes Leben" [Provoked life]:

"God is a substance, a drug!"

On the other hand, it is well known that substances like adrenaline, for example, are formed or set free in our organism by thoughts and emotions, which for their part determine the functions of the nervous system. One may therefore suppose that our material organism is susceptible to and shaped by our mind, in the same way that our intellectual essence is shaped by our biochemistry. Which came first can indeed no better be determined than the question, whether the chicken came before the egg.

In spite of my uncertainty with regard to the fundamental dangers that could lie in the use of hallucinogenic substances, I have continued investigations on the active principles of the Mexican magic morning glories, of which I wrote you briefly once before. In the seeds of this morning glory, that were called *ololiuhqui* by the ancient Aztecs, we found as active principles lysergic acid derivatives chemically very closely related to LSD. That was an almost unbelievable finding. I have all along had a particular love for the morning glories. They were the first flowers that I grew myself in my little child's garden. Their blue and red cups belong to the first memories of my childhood.

I recently read in a book by D. T. Suzuki, *Zen and Japanese Culture*, that the morning glory plays a great role in Japan, among the flower lovers, in literature, and in graphic arts. Its fleeting splendor has given the Japanese imagination rich stimulus. Among others, Suzuki quotes a three-line poem of the poetess

Chiyo (1702–75), who one morning went to fetch water from a neighbor's house, because . . .

"My trough is captivated
by a morning glory blossom,
So I ask after water."

The morning glory thus shows both possible ways of influencing the mind-body-essence of man: in Mexico it exerts its effects in a chemical way as a magic drug, while in Japan it acts from the spiritual side, through the beauty of its flower cups.

Wilflingen, 17 December 1961

Dear Mr. Hofmann,
I give you my thanks for your detailed letter of 16 December. I have reflected on your central question, and may probably become occupied with it on the occasion of the revision of *An der Zeitmauer* [At the wall of time]. There I intimated that, in the field of physics as well as in the field of biology, we are beginning to develop procedures that are no longer to be understood as advances in the established sense, but that rather intervene in evolution and lead forth in the development of the species. Certainly I turn the glove inside out, for I suppose that it is a new world age, which begins to act evolutionarily on the prototypes. Our science with its theories and discoveries is therefore not the cause, rather one of the consequences of evolution, among others. Animals, plants, the atmosphere and the surfaces of planets will be concerned

simultaneously. We do not progress from point to point, rather we cross over a line.

The risk that you indicated is well to be considered. However, it exists in every aspect of our existence. The common denominator appears now here, now there.

In mentioning radioactivity, you use the word *crack*. Cracks are not merely points of discovery, but also points of destruction. Compared to the effects of radiation, those of the magical drugs are more genuine and much less rough. In classical manner they lead us beyond the humane. Gurdjieff has already seen that to some extent. Wine has already changed much, has brought new gods and a new humanity with it. But wine is to the new substances as classical physics is to modern physics. These things should only be tried in small circles. I cannot agree with the thoughts of Huxley, that possibilities for transcendence could here be given to the masses. Indeed, this does not involve comforting fictions, but rather realities, if we take the matter earnestly. And few contacts will suffice here for the setting of courses and guidance. It also transcends theology and belongs in the chapter of theogony, as it necessarily entails entry into a new house, in the astrological sense. At first, one can be satisfied with this insight, and should above all be cautious with the designations.

Heartfelt thanks also for the beautiful picture of the blue morning glory. It appears to be the same that I cultivate year after year in my garden. I did not know that it possesses specific powers; however, that is probably the case with every plant. We do not know the key to most. Besides this, there must be a central viewpoint from which not only the chemistry, the structure, the color, but rather all attributes become significant. . . .

An Experiment with Psilocybin

Such theoretical discussions about the magic drugs were supplemented by practical experiments. One such experiment, which served as a comparison between LSD and psilocybin, took place in the spring of 1962. The proper occasion for it presented itself at the home of the Jüngers, in the former head forester's house of Stauffenberg's Castle in Wilflingen. My friends, the pharmacologist Professor Heribert Konzett and the Islamic scholar Dr. Rudolf Gelpke, also took part in this mushroom symposium.

The old chronicles described how the Aztecs drank *chocolatl* before they ate *teonanácatl*. Thus Mrs. Liselotte Jünger likewide served us hot chocolate, to set the mood. Then she abandoned the four men to their fate.

We had gathered in a fashionable living room, with a dark wooden ceiling, white tile stove, period furniture, old French engravings on the walls, a gorgeous bouquet of tulips on the table. Ernst Jünger wore a long, broad, dark blue striped kaftan-like garment that he had brought from Egypt; Heribert Konzett was resplendent in a brightly embroidered mandarin gown; Rudolf Gelpke and I had put on housecoats. The everyday reality should be laid aside, along with everyday clothing.

Shortly before sundown we took the drug, not the mushrooms, but rather their active principle, 20 mg psilocybin each. That corresponded to some two-thirds of the very strong dose that was taken by the *curandera* María Sabina in the form of *Psilocybe* mushrooms.

After an hour I still noticed no effect, while my companions were already very deeply into the trip. I had come with the hope that in the mushroom inebriation I could manage to allow certain images from euphoric moments of my childhood, which remained in my memory as blissful experiences, to come alive: a meadow covered with chrysanthemums lightly stirred by the early summer wind; the rosebush in the evening light after a rain storm; the blue irises hanging over the vineyard wall. Instead of these bright images from my childhood home, strange scenery emerged, when the mushroom factor finally began to act. Half stupefied, I sank deeper, passed through totally deserted cities with a Mexican type of exotic, yet dead splendor. Terrified, I tried to detain myself on the surface, to concentrate alertly on the óuter world, on the surroundings. For a time I succeeded. I then observed Ernst Jünger, colossal in the room, pacing back and forth, a powerful, mighty magician. Heribert Konzett in the silky lustrous housecoat seemed to be a dangerous, Chinese clown. Even Rudolf Gelpke appeared sinister to me; long, thin, mysterious.

With the increasing depth of inebriation, everything became yet stranger. I even felt strange to myself. Weird, cold, foolish, deserted, in a dull light, were the places I traversed when I closed my eyes. Emptied of all meaning, the environment also seemed ghostlike to me whenever I opened my eyes and tried to cling to the outer world. The total emptiness threatened to drag me down into absolute nothingness. I remember how I seized Rudolf Gelpke's arm as he passed by my chair, and held myself to him, in order not to sink into dark nothingness. Fear of death seized me, and illimitable longing to return to the living creation, to the reality of the world of men. After timeless fear I slowly returned to the room. I saw and heard the great magician lecturing uninterruptedly with a clear, loud voice, about Schopenhauer, Kant, Hegel, and speaking about the old Gäa, the beloved little mother. Heribert Konzett and Rudolf Gelpke were already completely on the earth again, while I could only regain my footing with great effort.

For me this entry into the mushroom world had been a test, a confrontation with a dead world and with the void. The experiment had developed differently from what I had expected. Nevertheless, the encounter with the void can also be appraised as a gain. Then the existence of the creation appears so much more wondrous.

Midnight had passed, as we sat together at the table that the mistress of the house had set in the upper story. We celebrated the return with an exquisite repast and with Mozart's music. The conversation, during which we exchanged our experiences, lasted almost until morning.

Ernst Jünger has described how he had experienced this trip, in his book *Annäherungen—Drogen und Rausch* [Approaches—drugs and inebriation] (published by Ernst Klett Verlag, Stuttgart, 1970), in the section "Ein Pilz-Symposium" [A mushroom symposium]. The following is an extract from the work:

> As usual, a half hour or a little more passed in silence. Then came the first signs: the flowers on the table began to flare up and sent out flashes. It was time for leaving work; outside the streets were being cleaned, like on every weekend. The brush strokes invaded the silence painfully. This shuffling and brushing, now

and again also a scraping, pounding, rumbling, and hammering, has random causes and is also symptomatic, like one of the signs that announces an illness. Again and again it also plays a role in the history of magic practices. . . .

By this time the mushroom began to act; the spring bouquet glowed darker. That was no natural light. The shadows stirred in the corners, as if they sought form. I became uneasy, even chilled, despite the heat that emanated from the tiles. I stretched myself on the sofa, drew the covers over my head.

Everything became skin and was touched, even the retina—there the contact was light. This light was multicolored; it arranged itself in strings, which gently swung back and forth; in strings of glass beads of oriental doorways. They formed doors, like those one passes through in a dream, curtains of lust and danger. The wind stirred them like a garment. They also fell down from the belts of dancers, opened and closed themselves with the swing of the hips, and from the beads a rippling of the most delicate sounds fluttered to the heightened senses. The chime of the silver rings on the ankles and wrists is already too loud. It smells of sweat, blood, tobacco, chopped horse hairs, cheap rose essence. Who knows what is going on in the stables?

It must be an immense palace, Mauritanian, not a good place. At this ballroom flights of adjoining rooms lead into the lower stratum. And everywhere the curtains with their glitter, their sparkling, radioactive glow. Moreover, the rippling of glassy instruments with their beckoning, their wooing solicitation: "Will you go with me, beautiful boy?" Now it ceased, now it repeated, more importunate, more intrusive, almost already assured of agreement.

Now came forms—historical collages, the *vox humana*, the call of the cuckoo. Was it the whore of Santa Lucia, who stuck her breasts out of the window? Then the play was ruined. Salome danced; the amber necklace emitted sparks and made the nipples erect. What would one not do for one's Johannes?*—damned, that was a disgusting obscenity, which did not come from me, but was whispered through the curtain.

The snakes were dirty, scarcely alive, they wallowed sluggishly over the floor mats. They were garnished with brilliant shards. Others looked up from the floor with red and green eyes. It glistened and whispered, hissed and sparkled like diminutive sickles at the sacred harvest. Then it quieted, and came anew, more faintly, more forward. They had me in their hand. "There we immediately understood ourselves."

Madam came through the curtain: she was busy, passed by me without noticing me. I saw the boots with the red heels. Garters constricted the thick thighs in the middle, the flesh bulged out there. The enormous breasts, the dark delta of the Amazon, parrots, piranhas, semiprecious stones everywhere.

Now she went into the kitchen—or are there still cellars here? The sparkling and whispering, the hissing and twinkling could no

*Translator's note: "Johannes" here is slang for penis, as in English "Dick" or "Peter."

166

longer be differentiated; it seemed to become concentrated, now proudly rejoicing, full of hope.

It became hot and intolerable; I threw the covers off. The room was faintly illuminated; the pharmacologist stood at the window in the white mandarin frock, which had served me shortly before in Rottweil at the carnival. The orientalist sat beside the tile stove; he moaned as if he had a nightmare. I understood; it had been a first round, and it would soon start again. The time was not yet up. I had already seen the beloved little mother under other circumstances. But even excrement is earth, belongs like gold to transformed matter. One must come to terms with it, without getting too close.

These were the earthy mushrooms. More light was hidden in the dark grain that burst from the ear, more yet in the green juice of the succulents on the glowing slopes of Mexico. . . .*

The trip had run awry—possibly I should address the mushrooms once more. Yet indeed the whispering returned, the flashing and sparkling—the bait pulled the fish close behind itself. Once the motif is given, then it engraves itself, like on a roller each new beginning, each new revolution repeats the melody. The game did not get beyond this kind of dreariness.

I don't know how often this was repeated, and prefer not to dwell upon it. Also, there are things which one would rather keep to oneself. In any case, midnight was past. . . .

*Translator's note: Jünger is referring to LSD, a derivative of ergot, and mescaline, derived from the Mexican *péyotl* cactus.

We went upstairs; the table was set. The senses were still heightened and the Doors of Perception were opened. The light undulated from the red wine in the carafe; a froth surged at the brim. We listened to a flute concerto. It had not turned out better for the others: How beautiful, to be back among men." Thus Albert Hofmann. . . .

The orientalist on the other hand had been in Samarkand, where Timur rests in a coffin of nephrite. He had followed the victorious march through cities, whose dowry on entry was a cauldron filled with eyes. There he had long stood before one of the skull pyramids that terrible Timur had erected, and in the multitude of severed heads had perceived even his own. It was encrusted with stones.

A light dawned on the pharmacologist when he heard this: Now I know why you were sitting in the armchair without your head—I was astonished; I knew I wasn't dreaming.

I wonder whether I should not strike out this detail since it borders on the area of ghost stories.

The mushroom substance had carried all four of us off, not into luminous heights, rather into deeper regions. It seems that the psilocybin inebriation is more darkly colored in the majority of cases than the inebriation produced by LSD. The influence of these two active substances is sure to differ from one individual to another. Personally, for me, there was more light in the LSD experiments than in the experiments with the earthy mushroom, just as Ernst Jünger remarks in the preceding report.

Another LSD Session

The next and last thrust into the inner universe together with Ernst Jünger, this time again using LSD, led us very far from everyday consciousness. We came close to the ultimate door. Of course this door, according to Ernst Jünger, will in fact only open for us in the great transition from life into the hereafter.

This last joint experiment occurred in February 1970, again at the head forester's house in Wilflingen. In this case there were only the two of us. Ernst Jünger took 0.15 mg LSD, I took 0.10 mg. Ernst Jünger has published without commentary the log book, the notes he made during the experiment, in *Approaches*, in the section "Nochmals LSD" [LSD once again]. They are scanty and tell the reader little, just like my own records.

The experiment lasted from morning just after breakfast until darkness fell. At the beginning of the trip, we again listened to the concerto for flute and harp by Mozart, which always made me especially happy, but this time, strange to say, seemed to me like the turning of porcelain figures. Then the intoxication led quickly into wordless depths. When I wanted to describe the perplexing alterations of consciousness to Ernst Jünger, no more than two or three words came out, for they sounded so false, so unable to express the experience; they seemed to originate from an infinitely distant world that had become strange; I abandoned the attempt, laughing hopelessly. Obviously, Ernst Jünger had the same experience, yet we did not need speech; a glance sufficed for the deepest understanding. I could, however, put some scraps of sentences on paper, such as at the beginning: "Our boat tosses violently." Later, upon regarding expensively bound books in the library: "Like red-gold pushed from within to without—exuding golden luster." Outside it began to snow. Masked children marched past and carts with carnival revelers passed by in the streets. With a glance through the window into the garden, in which snow patches lay, many-colored masks appeared over the high walls bordering it, embedded in an infinitely joyful shade of blue: "A Breughel garden—I live *with* and *in* the objects." Later: "At present—no connection with the everyday world." Toward the end, deep, comforting insight expressed: "Hitherto confirmed on my path." This time LSD had led to a blessed approach.

8

Meeting with Aldous Huxley

In the mid-1950s, two books by Aldous Huxley appeared, *The Doors of Perception* and *Heaven and Hell*, dealing with inebriated states produced by hallucinogenic drugs. The alterations of sensory perceptions and consciousness, which the author experienced in a self-experiment with mescaline, are skillfully described in these books. The mescaline experiment was a visionary experience for Huxley. He saw objects in a new light; they disclosed their inherent, deep, timeless existence, which remains hidden from everyday sight.

These two books contained fundamental observations on the essence of visionary experience and about the significance of this manner of comprehending the world—in cultural history, in the creation of myths, in the origin of religions, and in the creative process out of which works of art arise. Huxley saw the value of hallucinogenic drugs in that they give people who lack the gift of spontaneous visionary perception belonging to mystics, saints, and great artists, the potential to experience this extraordinary state of consciousness, and thereby to attain insight into the spiritual world of these great creators. Hallucinogens could lead to a deepened understanding of religious and mystical content, and to a new and fresh experience of the great works of art. For Huxley these drugs were keys capable of opening new doors of perception; chemical keys, in addition to other proven but laborious "door openers" to the visionary world like meditation, isolation, and fasting, or like certain yoga practices.

At the time I already knew the earlier work of this great writer and thinker, books that meant much to me, like *Point Counter Point, Brave New World, After Many a Summer, Eyeless in Gaza,* and a few others. In *The Doors of Perception* and *Heaven and Hell,* Huxley's newly-published works, I found a meaningful exposition of the experience induced by hallucinogenic drugs, and I thereby gained a deepened insight into my own LSD experiments.

I was therefore delighted when I received a telephone call from Aldous Huxley in the laboratory one morning in August 1961. He was passing through Zurich with his wife. He invited me and my wife to lunch in the Hotel Sonnenberg.

A gentleman with a yellow freesia in his buttonhole, a tall and noble appearance, who exuded kindness— this is the image I retained from this first meeting with Aldous Huxley. The table conversation revolved mainly around the problem of magic drugs. Both Huxley and his wife, Laura Archera Huxley, had also experimented with LSD and psilocybin. Huxley would have preferred not to designate these two substances and mescaline as "drugs," because in English usage, as also by the way with *Droge* in German, that word has a pejorative connotation, and because it was important to differentiate the hallucinogens from the other drugs, even linguistically. He believed in the great importance of agents producing visionary experience in the modern phase of human evolution.

He considered experiments under laboratory conditions to be insignificant, since in the extraordinarily intensified susceptibility and sensitivity to external impressions, the surroundings are of decisive importance. He recommended to my wife, when we spoke of her native place in the mountains, that she take LSD in an alpine meadow and then look into the blue cup of a gentian flower, to behold the wonder of creation.

As we parted, Aldous Huxley gave me, as a remembrance of this meeting, a tape recording of his lecture "Visionary Experience," which he had delivered the week before at an international congress on applied psychology in Copenhagen. In this lecture, Aldous Huxley spoke about the meaning and essence of visionary experience and compared this type of world view to the verbal and intellectual comprehension of reality as its essential complement.

In the following year, the newest and last book by Aldous Huxley appeared, the novel *Island*. This story, set on the utopian island Pala, is an attempt to blend the achievements of natural science and technical civilization with the wisdom of Eastern thought, to achieve a new culture in which rationalism and mysticism are fruitfully united. The *moksha* medicine, a magical drug prepared from a mushroom, plays a significant role in the life of the population of Pala (*moksha* is Sanskrit for "release," "liberation"). The drug could be used only in critical periods of life. The young men on Pala received it in initiation rites, it is dispensed to the protagonist of the novel during a life crisis, in the scope of a psychotherapeutic dialogue with a spiritual friend, and it helps the dying to relinquish the mortal body, in the transition to another existence.

In our conversation in Zurich, I had already learned

from Aldous Huxley that he would again treat the problem of psychedelic drugs in his forthcoming novel. Now he sent me a copy of *Island*, inscribed "To Dr. Albert Hofmann, the original discoverer of the *moksha* medicine, from Aldous Huxley."

The hopes that Aldous Huxley placed in psychedelic drugs as a means of evoking visionary experience, and the uses of these substances in everyday life, are subjects of a letter of 29 February 1962, in which he wrote me:

> . . . I have good hopes that this and similar work will result in the development of a real Natural History of visionary experience, in all its variations, determined by differences of physique, temperament and profession, and at the same time of a technique of Applied Mysticism—a technique for helping individuals to get the most out of their transcendental experience and to make use of the insights from the "Other World" in the affairs of "This World." Meister Eckhart wrote that "what is taken in by contemplation must be given out in love." Essentially this is what must be developed—the art of giving out in love and intelligence what is taken in from vision and the experience of self-transcendence and solidarity with the Universe. . . .

Aldous Huxley and I were together often at the annual convention of the World Academy of Arts and Sciences (WAAS) in Stockholm during late summer 1963. His suggestions and contributions to discussions at the sessions of the academy, through their form and importance, had a great influence on the proceedings. WAAS had been established in order to allow the most competent specialists to consider world problems in a forum free of ideological and religious restrictions and from an international viewpoint encompassing the whole world. The results: proposals, and thoughts in the form of appropriate publications, were to be placed at the disposal of the responsible governments and executive organizations.

The 1963 meeting of WAAS had dealt with the population explosion and the raw material reserves and food resources of the earth. The corresponding studies and proposals were collected in Volume II of WAAS under the title *The Population Crisis and the Use of World Resources*. A decade before birth control, environmental protection, and the energy crisis became catchwords, these world problems were examined there from the most serious point of view, and proposals for their solution were made to governments and responsible organizations. The catastrophic events since that time in the aforementioned fields makes evident the tragic discrepancy between recognition, desire, and feasibility.

Aldous Huxley made the proposal, as a continuation and complement of the theme "World Resources" at the Stockholm convention, to address the problem "Human Resources," the exploration and application of capabilities hidden in humans yet unused. A human race with more highly developed spiritual capacities, with expanded consciousness of the depth and the incomprehensible wonder of being, would also have greater understanding of and better consideration for the biological and material foundations of life on this earth. Above all, for Western people with their hypertrophied rationality, the development and expansion of a direct, emotional experience of reality, unobstructed by words and concepts, would be of evolutionary significance. Huxley considered

175

psychedelic drugs to be one means to achieve education in this direction. The psychiatrist Dr. Humphry Osmond, likewise participating in the congress, who had created the term *psychedelic* (mind-expanding), assisted him with a report about significant possibilities of the use of hallucinogens.

The convention in Stockholm in 1963 was my last meeting with Aldous Huxley. His physical appearance was already marked by a severe illness; his intellectual personage, however, still bore the undiminished signs of a comprehensive knowledge of the heights and depths of the inner and outer world of man, which he had displayed with so much genius, love, goodness, and humor in his literary work.

Aldous Huxley died on 22 November of the same year, on the same day President Kennedy was assassinated. From Laura Huxley I obtained a copy of her letter to Julian and Juliette Huxley, in which she reported to her brother- and sister-in-law about her husband's last day. The doctors had prepared her for a dramatic end, because the terminal phase of cancer of the throat, from which Aldous Huxley suffered, is usually accompanied by convulsions and choking fits. He died serenely and peacefully, however.

In the morning, when he was already so weak that he could no longer speak, he had written on a sheet of paper: "LSD—try it—intramuscular—100 mmg." Mrs. Huxley understood what was meant by this, and ignoring the misgivings of the attending physician, she gave him, with her own hand, the desired injection—she let him have the *moksha* medicine.

9

Correspondence with the Poet-Physician Walter Vogt

My friendship with the physician, psychiatrist, and writer Walter Vogt, M.D., is also among the personal contacts that I owe to LSD. As the following extract from our correspondence shows, it was less the medicinal aspects of LSD, important to the physician, than the consciousness-altering effects on the depth of the psyche, of interest to the writer, that constituted the theme of our correspondence.

Muri/Bern, 22 November 1970

Dear Mr. Hofmann,

Last night I dreamed that I was invited to tea in a cafe by a friendly family in Rome. This family also knew the pope, and so the pope sat at the same table to tea with us. He was all in white and also wore a white miter. He sat there so handsome and was silent.

And today I suddenly had the idea of sending you my *Vogel auf dem Tisch* [Bird on the table]—as a visiting card if you so wish—a book that remained a little apocryphal, which upon reflection I do not regret, although the Italian translator is firmly convinced that is my best. (Ah yes, the pope is also an Italian. So it goes. . . .)

Possibly this little work will interest you. It was written in 1966 by an author who at that time still had not had any shred of experience with psychedelic substances and who read the reports about medicinal experiments with these drugs devoid of understanding. However, little has changed since, except that now the misgiving comes from the other side.

I suppose that your discovery has caused a hiatus (not directly a Saul-to-Paul conversion as Roland Fischer says . . .) in my work (also a large word)—and indeed, that which I have written since has become rather realistic or at least less expressive. In any case I could not have brought off the cool realism of my TV piece "Spiele der Macht" [Games of power] without it. The different drafts attest it, in case they are still lying around somewhere.

Should you have interest and time for a meeting, it would delight me very much to visit you sometime for a conversation.

W. V.

Burg, i.L. 28 November 1970

Dear Mr. Vogt,

If the bird that alighted on my table was able to find its way to me, this is one more debt I owe to the magical effect of LSD. I could soon write a book about all of the results that derive from that experiment in 1943. . . .

A. H.

Dear Mr. Hofmann,
Enclosed is a critique of Jünger's
Annäherungen [Approaches], from the daily
paper, that will presumably interest you. . . .
It seems to me that to hallucinate—to
dream—to write, stands at all times in contrast
to everyday consciousness, and their functions
are complementary. Here I can naturally speak
only for myself. This could be different with
others—it is also truly difficult to speak with
others about such things, because people often
speak altogether different languages. . . .
However, since you are now gathering
autographs, and do me the honor of
incorporating some of my letters in your
collection, I enclose for you the manuscript of
my "testament"—in which your discovery
plays a role as "the only joyous invention of the
twentieth century. . . ."

W. V.

dr. walter vogts most recent testament 1969
I wish to have no special funeral
only expensive and obscene orchids
innumerable little birds with gay names
no naked dancers
but
psychedelic garments
loudspeaker in every corner and
nothing but the latest beatles record*
one hundred thousand million times
and

*Abbey Road

179

do what you like**
on an endless tape
nothing more
than a popular Christ with a halo of genuine
    gold
and a beloved mourning congregation
that pumped themselves full with acid***
till they go to heaven****
one two three four five six seven
possibly we will encounter one another there

> most cordially dedicated
> to Dr. Albert Hofmann
> Beginning of Spring 1971

> Burg i.L., 29 March 1971

Dear Mr. Vogt,

You have again presented me with a lovely
letter and a very valuable autograph, the
testament 1969. . . .

Very remarkable dreams in recent times
induce me to test a connection between the
composition (chemical) of the evening meal
and the quality of dreams. Yes, LSD is also
something that one eats. . . .

> A. H.

> Muri/Bern, 5 September 1971

Dear Mr. Hofmann,

Over the weekend at Murtensee* I often
thought of you—a most radiant autumn day.
Yesterday, Saturday, thanks to one tablet of

**"Blind Faith"
***acid = LSD
****From Abbey Road, side two
*On that Sunday, I (A. H.) hovered over the Murtensee in the balloon of my
friend E. I., who had taken me along as passenger.

180

aspirin (on account of a headache or mild flu), I experienced a very comical flashback, like with mescaline (of which I have had only a little, exactly once). . . .

I have read a delightful essay by Wasson about mushrooms; he divides mankind into mycophobes and mycophiles. . . . Lovely fly agarics must now be growing in the forest near you. Sometime shouldn't we sample some?

W. V.

Muri/Bern, 7 September 1971

Dear Mr. Hofmann,

Now I feel I must write briefly to tell you what I have done outside in the sun, on the dock under your balloon: I finally wrote some notes about our visit in Villars-sur-Ollons (with Dr. Leary), then a hippie-bark went by on the lake, self-made like from a Fellini film, which I sketched, and over and above it I drew your balloon. . . .

W. V.

Burg i.L., 15 April 1972

Dear Mr. Vogt,

Your television play "Spiele der Macht" [Games of power] has impressed me extraordinarily. . . .

I congratulate you on this magnificent piece, which allows mental cruelty to become conscious, and therefore also acts in its way as "consciousness-expanding", and can thereby prove itself therapeutic in a higher sense, like ancient tragedy.

A. H.

Dear Mr. Vogt,

Now I have already read your lay sermon three times, the description and interpretation of your Sinai Trip.* Was it really an LSD trip? . . . It was a courageous deed, to choose such a notorious event as a drug experience as the theme of a sermon, even a lay sermon. But the questions raised by hallucinogenic drugs do actually belong in the church—in a prominent place in the church, for they are sacred drugs (péyotl, teonanácatl, ololiuhqui, with which LSD is mostly closely related by chemical structure and activity).

I can fully agree with what you say in your introduction about the modern ecclesiastical religiosity: the three sanctioned states of consciousness (the waking condition of uninterrupted work and performance of duty, alcoholic intoxication, and sleep), the distinction between two phases of psychedelic inebriation (the first phase, the peak of the trip, in which the cosmic relationship is experienced, or the submersion into one's own body, in which everything that is, is within; and the second phase, characterized as the

*Walter Vogt: Mein Sinai Trip. Eine Laienpredigt [My Sinai trip: A lay sermon] (Verlag der Arche, Zürich, 1972). This publication contains the text of a lay sermon that Walter Vogt gave on 14 November 1971 on the invitation of Parson Christoph Möhl, in the Protestant church of Vaduz (Lichtenstein), in the course of a series of sermons by writers, and in addition contains an afterword by the author and by the inviting parson. It involves the description and interpretation of an ecstatic-religious experience evoked by LSD, that the author is able to "place in a distant, if you will superficial, analogy to the great Sinai Trip of Moses." It is not only the "patriarchal atmosphere" that is to be traced out of these descriptions, that constitutes this analogy; there are deeper references, which are more to be read between the lines of this text.

phase of enhanced comprehension of symbols), and the allusion to the candor that hallucinogens bring about in consciousness states. These are all observations that are of fundamental importance in the judgement of hallucinogenic inebriation.

The most worthwhile spiritual benefit from LSD experiments was the experience of the inextricable intertwining of the physical and spiritual. "Christ in matter" (Teilhard de Chardin). Did the insight first come to you also through your drug experiences, that we must descend "into the flesh, which we are," in order to get new prophesies?

A criticism of your sermon: you allow the "deepest experience that there is"—"The kingdom of heaven is within you"—to be uttered by Timothy Leary. This sentence, quoted without the indication of its true source, could be interpreted as ignorance of one, or rather *the* principal truth of Christian belief.

One of your statements deserves universal recognition: "There is no non-ecstatic religious experience." . . .

Next Monday evening I shall be interviewed on Swiss television (about LSD and the Mexican magic drugs, on the program "At First Hand"). I am curious about the sort of questions that will be asked. . .

A. H.

Muri/Bern, 24 May 1973

Dear Mr. Hofmann,

Of course it was LSD—only I did not want to write about it explicitly, I really do not know just why myself. . . . The great emphasis I placed on the good Leary, who now seems to me to be somewhat flipped out, as the prime witness, can indeed only be explained by the special context of the talk or sermon.

I must admit that the perception that we must descend "into the flesh, which we are" actually first came to me with LSD. I still ruminate on it, possibly it even came "too late" for me in fact, although more and more I advocate your opinion that LSD should be taboo for youth (taboo, not forbidden, that is the difference . . .).

The sentence that you like, "there is no nonecstatic religious experience," was apparently not liked so much by others—for example, by my (almost only) literary friend and minister-lyric poet Kurt Marti. . . . But in any case, we are practically never of the same opinion about anything, and notwithstanding, we constitute when we occasionally communicate by phone and arrange little activities together, the smallest minimafia of Switzerland. . . .

W. V.

Burg i.L., 13 April 1974

Dear Mr. Vogt,

Full of suspense, we watched your TV play "Pilate before the Silent Christ" yesterday evening.

. . . as a representation of the fundamental man-God relationship: man, who comes to God with his most difficult questions, which finally he must answer himself, because God is silent. He does not answer them with *words*. The answers are contained in the book of his creation (to which the questioning man himself belongs). *True* natural science=deciphering of this text.   .   .   .

A. H.

Muri/Bern, 11 May 1974

Dear Mr. Hofmann,

I have composed a "poem" in half twilight, that I dare to send to you. At first I wanted to send it to Leary, but this would make no sense.

> Leary in jail
> Gelpke is dead
> Treatment in the asylum
> is this your psychedelic
> revolution?
> Had we
> taken seriously something
> with which one only ought to play
> or
> vice-versa . . .

W. V.

10

Various Visitors

The diverse aspects, the multi-faceted emanations of LSD are also expressed in the variety of cultural circles with which this substance has brought me into contact. On the scientific plane, this has involved colleagues—chemists, pharmacologists, physicians, and mycologists—whom I met at universities, congresses, lectures, or with whom I came into association through publication. In the literary-philosophical field there were contacts with writers. In the preceding chapters I have reported on the relationships of this type that were most significant for me. LSD also provided me with a variegated series of personal acquaintances from the drug scene and from hippie circles, which will briefly be described here.

Most of these visitors came from the United States and were young people, often in transit to the Far East in search of Eastern wisdom or of a guru; or else hoping to come by drugs more easily there. Prague also was sometimes the goal, because LSD of good quality could at the time easily be acquired there.* Once ar-

*Translator's Note: When Sandoz's patents on LSD expired in 1963, the Czech pharmaceutical firm Spofa began to manufacture the drug.

rived in Europe, they wanted to take advantage of the opportunity to see the father of LSD, "the man who made the famous LSD bicycle trip." But more serious concerns sometimes motivated a visit. There was the desire to report on personal LSD experiences and to debate the purport of their meaning, at the source, so to speak. Only rarely did a visit prove to be inspired by the desire to obtain LSD when a visitor hinted that he or she wished once to experiment with most assuredly pure material, with original LSD.

Visitors of various types and with diverse desires also came from Switzerland and other European countries. Such encounters have become rarer in recent times, which may be related to the fact that LSD has become less important in the drug scene. Whenever possible, I have welcomed such visitors or agreed to meet somewhere. This I considered to be an obligation connected with my role in the history of LSD, and I have tried to help by instructing and advising.

Sometimes no true conversation occurred, for example with the inhibited young man who arrived on a motorbike. I was not clear about the objective of his visit. He stared at me, as if asking himself: can the man who has made something so weird as LSD really look so completely ordinary? With him, as with other similar visitors, I had the feeling that he hoped, in my presence, the LSD riddle would somehow solve itself.

Other meetings were completely different, like the one with the young man from Toronto. He invited me to lunch at an exclusive restaurant—impressive appearance, tall, slender, a businessman, proprietor of an important industrial firm in Canada, brilliant intellect. He thanked me for the creation of LSD, which had given his life another direction. He had been 100 percent a businessman, with a purely materialistic world view. LSD had opened his eyes to the spiritual aspect of life. Now he possessed a sense for art, literature, and philosophy and was deeply concerned with religious and metaphysical questions. He now desired to make the LSD experience accessible in a suitable milieu to his young wife, and hoped for a similarly fortunate transformation in her.

Not as profound, yet still liberating and rewarding, were the results of LSD experiments which a young Dane described to me with much humor and fantasy. He came from California, where he had been a houseboy for Henry Miller in Big Sur. He moved on to France with the plan of acquiring a dilapidated farm there, which he, a skilled carpenter, then wanted to restore himself. I asked him to obtain an autograph of his former employer for my collection, and after some time I actually received an original piece of writing from Henry Miller's hand.

A young woman sought me out to report on LSD experiences that had been of great significance to her inner development. As a superficial teenager who pursued all sorts of entertainments, and quite neglected by her parents, she had begun to take LSD out of curiosity and love of adventure. For three years she took frequent LSD trips. They led to an astonishing intensification of her inner life. She began to seek after the deeper meaning of her existence, which eventually revealed itself to her. Then, recognizing that LSD had no further power to help her, without difficulty or exertion of will she was able to abandon the drug. Thereafter she was in a position to develop herself further without artificial means. She was now a happy intrinsically secure person—thus she concluded her report. This young woman had decided to tell me her history, because she supposed that I was often attacked by narrow-minded persons who saw only the damage that LSD sometimes caused among youths. The immediate motive of her testimony was a conversation that she had accidentally overheard on a railway journey. A man complained about me, finding it disgraceful that I had spoken on the LSD problem in an interview published in the newspaper. In his opinion, I ought to denounce LSD as primarily the devil's work and should publicly admit my guilt in the matter.

Persons in LSD delirium, whose condition could have given rise to such indignant condemnation, have never personally come into my sight. Such cases, attributable to LSD consumption under irresponsible circumstances, to overdosage, or to psychotic predisposition, always landed in the hospital or at the police station. Great publicity always came their way.

A visit by one young American girl stands out in my memory as an example of the tragic effects of LSD. It was during the lunch hour, which I normally spent in my office under strict confinement—no visitors, secretary's office closed up. Knocking came at the door, discretely but firmly repeated, until eventually I went to open it. I scarcely believed my eyes: before me stood a very beautiful young woman, blond, with large blue eyes, wearing a long hippie dress, headband, and sandals. "I am Joan, I come from New York—you are Dr. Hofmann?" Before I inquired what brought her to me, I asked her how she had got through the two checkpoints, at the main entrance to the factory area and at the door of the laboratory building, for visitors were admitted only after telephone query, and this flower child must have been especially noticeable. "I am an angel, I can pass everywhere," she replied. Then she explained that she came on a great mission. She had to rescue her country, the United States; above all she had to direct the president (at the time L. B.

Johnson) onto the correct path. This could be accomplished only by having him take LSD. Then he would receive the good ideas that would enable him to lead the country out of war and internal difficulties.

Joan had come to me hoping that I would help her fulfill her mission, namely to give LSD to the president. Her name would indicate she was the Joan of Arc of the USA. I don't know whether my arguments, advanced with all consideration of her holy zeal, were able to convince her that her plan had no prospects of success on psychological, technical, internal, and external grounds. Disappointed and sad she went away. Next day I received a telephone call from Joan. She again asked me to help her, since her financial resources were exhausted. I took her to a friend in Zurich who provided her with work, and with whom she could live. Joan was a teacher by profession, and also a nightclub pianist and singer. For a while she played and sang in a fashionable Zurich restaurant. The good bourgeois clients of course had no idea what sort of angel sat at the grand piano in a black evening dress and entertained them with sensitive playing and a soft and sensuous voice. Few paid attention to the words of her songs; they were for the most part hippie songs, many of them containing veiled praise of drugs. The Zurich performance did not last long; within a few weeks I learned from my friend that Joan had suddenly disappeared. He received a greeting card from her three months later, from Israel. She had been committed to a psychiatric hospital there.

For the conclusion of my assortment of LSD visitors, I wish to report about a meeting in which LSD figured only indirectly. Miss H.S., head secretary in a hospital, wrote to ask me for a personal interview. She came to tea. She explained her visit thus: in a report about an LSD experience, she had read the description of a condition she herself had experienced as a young girl, which still disturbed her today; possibly I could help her to understand this experience.

She had gone on a business trip as a commercial apprentice. They spent the night in a mountain hotel. H. S. awoke very early and left the house alone in order to watch the sunrise. As the mountains began to light up in a sea of rays, she was perfused by an unprecedented feeling of happiness, which persisted even after she joined the other participants of the trip at morning service in the chapel. During the Mass everything appeared to her in a supernatural luster, and the feeling of happiness intensified to such an extent that she had to cry loudly. She was brought back to the hotel and treated as someone with a mental disorder.

This experience largely determined her later personal life. H.S. feared she was not completely normal. On the one hand, she feared this experience, which had been explained to her as a nervous breakdown; on the other hand, she longed for a repetition of the condition. Internally split, she had led an unstable life. In repeated vocational changes and in varying personal relationships, consciously or unconsciously she again sought this ecstatic outlook, which once made her so deeply happy.

I was able to reassure my visitor. It was no psychopathological event, no nervous breakdown that she had experienced at the time. What many people seek to attain with the help of LSD, the visionary experience of a deeper reality, had come to her as spontaneous grace. I recommended a book by Aldous Huxley to her, *The Perennial Philosophy* (Harper, New York & London, 1945) a collection of reports of spontaneous blessed visions from all times and cultures. Huxley wrote that not only mystics and saints, but also many more ordinary people than one generally supposes, experience such blessed moments, but that most do not recognize their importance and, instead of regarding them as promising rays of hope, repress them, because they do not fit into everyday rationality.

11

LSD Experience and Reality

*Was kann ein Mensch im Leben mehr
gewinnen
Als dass sich Gott-Natur ihm offenbare?*

*What more can a person gain in life
Than that God-Nature reveals himself to
him?*

Goethe

I am often asked what has made the deepest impression upon me in my LSD experiments, and whether I have arrived at new understandings through these experiences.

Various Realities

Of greatest significance to me has been the insight that I attained as a fundamental understanding from all of my LSD experiments: what one commonly takes as "the reality," including the reality of one's own individual person, by no means signifies something fixed, but rather something that is ambiguous—that there is not only one, but that there are many realities, each comprising also a different consciousness of the ego.

One can also arrive at this insight through scientific reflections. The problem of reality is and has been from time immemorial a central concern of philosophy. It is, however, a fundamental distinction, whether one approaches the problem of reality rationally, with the logical methods of philosophy, or if one obtrudes upon this problem emotionally, through an existential experience. The first planned LSD experiment was therefore so deeply moving and alarming, because everyday reality and the ego experiencing it, which I had until then considered to be the only reality, dissolved, and an unfamiliar ego experienced another, unfamiliar reality. The problem concerning the innermost self also appeared, which, itself unmoved, was able to record these external and internal transformations.

Reality is inconceivable without an experiencing subject, without an ego. It is the product of the exterior world, of the sender and of a receiver, an ego in whose deepest self the emanations of the exterior world, registered by the antennae of the sense organs, become conscious. If one of the two is lacking, no reality happens, no radio music plays, the picture screen remains blank.

If one continues with the conception of reality as a product of sender and receiver, then the entry of another reality under the influence of LSD may be explained by the fact that the brain, the seat of the receiver, becomes biochemically altered. The receiver is thereby tuned into another wavelength than that corresponding to normal, everyday reality. Since the endless variety and diversity of the universe correspond to infinitely many different wavelengths, depending on the adjustment of the receiver, many different realities, including the respective ego, can become conscious. These different realities, more correctly designated as different aspects of *the* reality, are not mutually exclusive but are complementary, and form together a portion of the all-encompassing, timeless, transcendental reality, in which even the unimpeachable core of self-consciousness, which has the power to record the different egos, is located.

The true importance of LSD and related hallucinogens lies in their capacity to shift the wavelength setting of the receiving "self," and thereby to evoke alterations in reality consciousness. This ability to allow different, new pictures of reality to arise, this truly cosmogonic power, makes the cultish worship of hallucinogenic plants as sacred drugs understandable.

What constitutes the essential, characteristic difference between everyday reality and the world picture experienced in LSD inebriation? Ego and the outer world are separated in the normal condition of consciousness, in everyday reality; one stands face-to-face with the outer world; it has become an object. In the LSD state the boundaries between the experiencing self and the outer world more or less disappear, depending on the depth of the inebriation. Feedback between receiver and sender takes place. A portion of the self overflows into the outer world, into objects, which begin to live, to have another, a deeper meaning. This can be perceived as a blessed, or as a demonic transformation imbued with terror, proceeding to a loss of the trusted ego. In an auspicious case, the new ego feels blissfully united with the objects of the outer world and consequently also with its fellow beings. This experience of deep oneness with the exterior world can even intensify to a feeling of the self being one with the universe. This condition of cosmic consciousness, which under favorable conditions can be evoked by LSD or by another hallucinogen from the group of Mexican sacred drugs, is analogous to spontaneous religious enlightenment, with the *unio mystica*. In both conditions, which often last only for a timeless moment, a reality is experienced that exposes a gleam of the transcendental reality, in which universe and self, sender and receiver, are one.*

Gottfried Benn, in his essay "Provoziertes Leben" [Provoked life] (in *Ausdruckswelt*, Limes Verlag, Wiesbaden, 1949), characterized the reality in which self and world are separated, as "the schizoid catastrophe, the Western entelechy neurosis." He further writes:

> . . . In the southern part of our continent this concept of reality began to be formed. The Hellenistic-European agonistic principle of victory through effort, cunning, malice, talent, force, and later, European Darwinism and "superman," was instrumental in its formation. The ego emerged, dominated, fought; for this it needed instruments, material, power. It had a different relationship to matter, more removed sensually, but closer formally. It analyzed matter, tested, sorted: weapons, object of exchange, ransom money. It clarified matter through isolation, reduced it to formulas, took pieces out of it, divided it up. [Matter became] a concept which hung like a disaster over the West, with which the West fought, without grasping it, to which it

*The relationship of spontaneous to drug-induced enlightenment has been most extensively investigated by R. C. Zaehner, *Mysticism—Sacred and Profane* (The Clarendon Press, Oxford, 1957).

sacrified enormous quantities of blood and happiness; a concept whose inner tension and fragmentations it was impossible to dissolve through a natural viewing or methodical insight into the inherent unity and peace of prelogical forms of being . . . instead the cataclysmic character of this idea became clearer and clearer . . . a state, a social organization, a public morality, for which life is economically usable life and which does not recognize the world of provoked life, cannot stop its destructive force. A society, whose hygiene and race cultivation as a modern ritual is founded solely on hollow biological statistics, can only represent the external viewpoint of the mass; for this point of view it can wage war, incessantly, for reality is simply raw material, but its metaphysical background remains forever obscured.*

As Gottfried Benn formulates it in these sentences, a concept of reality that separates self and the world has decisively determined the evolutionary course of European intellectual history. Experience of the world as matter, as object, to which man stands opposed, has produced modern natural science and technology—creations of the Western mind that have changed the world. With their help human beings have subdued the world. Its wealth has been exploited in a manner that may be characterized as plundering, and the sublime accomplishment of technological civilization, the comfort of Western industrial society, stands face-

*This excerpt from Benn's essay was taken from Ralph Metzner's translation "Provoked Life: An Essay on the Anthropology of the Ego," which was published in *Psychedelic Review* 1 (1): 47–54, 1963. Minor corrections in Metzner's text have been made by A. H.

to-face with a catastrophic destruction of the environment. Even to the heart of matter, to the nucleus of the atom and its splitting, this objective intellect has progressed and has unleashed energies that threaten all life on our planet.

A misuse of knowledge and understanding, the products of searching intelligence, could not have emerged from a consciousness of reality in which human beings are not separated from the environment but rather exist as part of living nature and the universe. All attempts today to make amends for the damage through environmentally protective measures must remain only hopeless, superficial patchwork, if no curing of the "Western entelechy neurosis" ensues, as Benn has characterized the objective reality conception. Healing would mean existential experience of a deeper, self-encompassing reality.

The experience of such a comprehensive reality is impeded in an environment rendered dead by human hands, such as is present in our great cities and industrial districts. Here the contrast between self and outer world becomes especially evident. Sensations of alienation, of loneliness, and of menace arise. It is these sensations that impress themselves on everyday consciousness in Western industrial society; they also take the upper hand everywhere that technological civilization extends itself, and they largely determine the production of modern art and literature.

There is less danger of a cleft reality experience arising in a natural environment. In field and forest, and in the animal world sheltered therein, indeed in every garden, a reality is perceptible that is infinitely more real, older, deeper, and more wondrous than everything made by people, and that will yet endure, when the inanimate, mechanical, and concrete world again vanishes, becomes rusted and fallen into ruin. In the sprouting, growth, blooming, fruiting, death, and regermination of plants, in their relationship with the sun, whose light they are able to convert into chemically bound energy in the form of organic compounds, out of which all that lives on our earth is built; in the being of plants the same mysterious, inexhaustible, eternal life energy is evident that has also brought us forth and takes us back again into its womb, and in which we are sheltered and united with all living things.

We are not leading up to a sentimental enthusiasm for nature, to "back to nature" in Rousseau's sense. That romantic movement, which sought the idyll in nature, can also be explained by a feeling of humankind's separation from nature. What is needed today is a fundamental reexperience of the oneness of all living things, a comprehensive reality consciousness that ever more infrequently develops spontaneously, the more the primordial flora and fauna of our mother earth must yield to a dead technological environment.

Mystery and Myth

The notion of reality as the self juxtaposed to the world, in confrontation with the outer world, began to form itself, as reported in the citation from Benn, in the southern portion of the European continent in Greek antiquity. No doubt people at that time knew the suffering that was connected with such a cleft reality consciousness. The Greek genius tried the cure, by supplementing the multiformed and richly colored, sensual as well as deeply sorrowful Apollonian world view created by the subject/object cleavage, with the Dionysian world of experience, in which this cleavage is abolished in ecstatic inebriation. Nietzsche writes in *The Birth of Tragedy:*

201

It is either through the influence of narcotic potions, of which all primitive peoples and races speak in hymns, or through the powerful approach of spring, penetrating with joy all of nature, that those Dionysian stirrings arise, which in their intensification lead the individual to forget himself completely. . . . Not only does the bond between man and man come to be forged once again by the magic of the Dionysian rite, but alienated, hostile, or subjugated nature again celebrates her reconciliation with her prodigal son, man.

The Mysteries of Eleusis, which were celebrated annually in the fall, over an interval of approximately 2,000 years, from about 1500 B.C. until the fourth century A.D., were intimately connected with the ceremonies and festivals in honor of the god Dionysus. These Mysteries were established by the goddess of agriculture, Demeter, as thanks for the recovery of her daughter Persephone, whom Hades, the god of the underworld, had abducted. A further thank offering was the ear of grain, which was presented by the two goddesses to Triptolemus, the first high priest of Eleusis. They taught him the cultivation of grain, which Triptolemus then disseminated over the whole globe. Persephone, however, was not always allowed to remain with her mother, because she had taken nourishment from Hades, contrary to the order of the highest gods. As punishment she had to return to the underworld for a part of the year. During this time, it was winter on the earth, the plants died and were withdrawn into the ground, to awaken to new life early in the year with Persephone's journey to earth.

The myth of Demeter, Persephone, Hades, and the other gods, which was enacted as a drama, formed, however, only the external framework of events. The climax of the yearly ceremonies, which began with a procession from Athens to Eleusis lasting several days, was the concluding ceremony with the initiation, which took place in the night. The initiates were forbidden by penalty of death to divulge what they had learned, beheld, in the innermost, holiest chamber of the temple, the *telesterion* (goal). Not one of the multitude that were initiated into the secret of Eleusis has ever done this. Pausanias, Plato, many Roman emperors like Hadrian and Marcus Aurelius, and many other known personages of antiquity were party to this initiation. It must have been an illumination, a visionary glimpse of a deeper reality, an insight into the true basis of the universe. That can be concluded from the statements of initiates about the value, about the importance of the vision. Thus it is reported in a Homeric Hymn: "Blissful is he among men on Earth, who has beheld that! He who has not been initiated into the holy Mysteries, who has had no part therein, remains a corpse in gloomy darkness." Pindar speaks of the Eleusinian benediction with the following words: "Blissful is he, who after having beheld this enters on the way beneath the Earth. He knows the end of life as well as its divinely granted beginning." Cicero, also a famous initiate, likewise put in first position the splendor that fell upon his life from Eleusis, when he said: "Not only have we received the reason there, that we may live in joy, but also, besides, that we may die with better hope."

How could the mythological representation of such an obvious occurrence, which runs its course annually before our eyes—the seed grain that is dropped into the earth, dies there, in order to allow a new plant, new life, to ascend into the light—prove to be such a deep, comforting experience as that attested by the cited reports? It is traditional knowledge that the initiates were furnished with a potion, the *kykeon*, for the final ceremony. It is also known that barley extract and mint were ingredients of the *kykeon*. Religious scholars and scholars of mythology, like Karl Kerényi, from whose book on the Eleusinian Mysteries (Rhein-Verlag, Zürich, 1962) the preceding statements were taken, and with whom I was associated in relation to the research on this mysterious potion,* are of the opinion that the *kykeon* was mixed with an hallucinogenic drug.** That would make understandable the ecstatic-visionary experience of the Demeter-Persephone myth, as a symbol of the cycle of life and death in both a comprehensive and timeless reality.

When the Gothic king Alarich, coming from the north, invaded Greece in 396 A.D. and destroyed the sanctuary of Eleusis, it was not only the end of a religious center, but it also signified the decisive downfall of the ancient world. With the monks that accompanied Alarich, Christianity penetrated into the country that must be regarded as the cradle of European culture.

The cultural-historical meaning of the Eleusinian Mysteries, their influence on European intellectual history, can scarcely be overestimated. Here suffering humankind found a cure for its rational, objective, cleft intellect, in a mystical totality experience, that let it believe in immortality, in an everlasting existence.

This belief had survived in early Christianity, al-

---

*In the English publication of Kerényi's book *Eleusis* (Schocken Books, New York, 1977) a reference is made to this collaboration.
**In *The Road to Eleusis* by R. Gordon Wasson, Albert Hofmann, and Carl A. P. Ruck (Harcourt Brace Jovanovich, New York, 1978) the possibility is discussed that the *kykeon* could have acted through an LSD-like preparation of ergot.

though with other symbols. It is found as a promise, even in particular passages of the Gospels, most clearly in the Gospel according to John, as in Chapter 14: 16–20. Jesus speaks to his disciples, as he takes leave of them:

> And I will pray the Father, and he shall give you another Comforter, that he may abide with you forever;
> *Even the Spirit of truth;* whom the world cannot receive, because it seeth him not, neither knoweth him: but ye know him; for he dwelleth with you, and shall be in you.
> I will not leave you comfortless: I will come to you. Yet a little while, and the world seeth me no more; but ye see me: because I live, ye shall live also.
> *At that day ye shall know that I am in my Father, and ye in me, and I in you.*

This promise constitutes the heart of my Christian beliefs and my call to natural-scientific research: we will attain to knowledge of the universe through the spirit of truth, and thereby to understanding of our being one with the deepest, most comprehensive reality, God.

Ecclesiastical Christianity, determined by the duality of creator and creation, has, however, with its nature-alienated religiosity largely obliterated the Eleusinian-Dionysian legacy of antiquity. In the Christian sphere of belief, only special blessed men have attested to a timeless, comforting reality, experienced in a spontaneous vision, an experience to which in antiquity the elite of innumerable generations had access through the initiation at Eleusis. The *unio mystica* of Catholic saints and the visions that the representatives of Christian mysticism—Jakob Boehme, Meister Eckhart, Angelus Silesius, Thomas Traherne, William Blake, and others—describe in their writings, are obviously essentially related to the enlightenment that the initiates to the Eleusinian Mysteries experienced.

The fundamental importance of a mystical experience, for the recovery of people in Western industrial societies who are sickened by a one-sided, rational, materialistic world view, is today given primary emphasis, not only by adherents to Eastern religious movements like Zen Buddhism, but also by leading representatives of academic psychiatry. Of the appropriate literature, we will here refer only to the books of Balthasar Staehelin, the Basel psychiatrist working in Zürich.* They make reference to numerous other authors who deal with the same problem. Today a type of "metamedicine," "metapsychology," and "metapsychiatry" is beginning to call upon the metaphysical element in people, which manifests itself as an experience of a deeper, duality-surmounting reality, and to make this element a basic healing principle in therapeutic practice.

In addition, it is most significant that not only medicine but also wider circles of our society consider the overcoming of the dualistic, cleft world view to be a prerequisite and basis for the recovery and spiritual renewal of occidental civilization and culture. This renewal could lead to the renunciation of the materialistic philosophy of life and the development of a new reality consciousness.

As a path to the perception of a deeper, comprehensive reality, in which the experiencing individual is

*Haben und Sein (1969), Die Welt als Du (1970), Urvertrauen und zweite Wirklichkeit (1973), and Der finale Mensch (1976); all published by Theologischer Verlag, Zürich.

also sheltered, meditation, in its different forms, occupies a prominent place today. The essential difference between meditation and prayer in the usual sense, which is based upon the duality of creator-creation, is that meditation aspires to the abolishment of the I-you-barrier by a fusing of object and subject, of sender and receiver, of objective reality and self.

Objective reality, the world view produced by the spirit of scientific inquiry, is the myth of our time. It has replaced the ecclesiastical-Christian and myth-ical-Apollonian world view.

But this ever broadening factual knowledge, which constitutes objective reality, need not be a desecration. On the contrary, if it only advances deep enough, it inevitably leads to the inexplicable, primal ground of the universe: the wonder, the mystery of the divine—in the microcosm of the atom, in the macrocosm of the spiral nebula; in the seeds of plants, in the body and soul of people.

Meditation begins at the limits of objective reality, at the farthest point yet reached by rational knowledge and perception. Meditation thus does not mean rejection of objective reality; on the contrary, it consists of a penetration to deeper dimensions of reality. It is not escape into an imaginary dream world; rather it seeks after the comprehensive truth of objective reality, by simultaneous, stereoscopic contemplation of its surfaces and depths.

It could become of fundamental importance, and be not merely a transient fashion of the present, if more and more people today would make a daily habit of devoting an hour, or at least a few minutes, to meditation. As a result of the meditative penetration and broadening of the natural-scientific world view, a new, deepened reality consciousness would have to evolve, which would increasingly become the property of all humankind. This could become the basis of a new religiosity, which would not be based on belief in the dogmas of various religions, but rather on perception through the "spirit of truth." What is meant here is a perception, a reading and understanding of the text at first hand, "out of the book that God's finger has written" (Paracelsus), out of the creation.

The transformation of the objective world view into a deepened and thereby religious reality consciousness can be accomplished gradually, by continuing practice of meditation. It can also come about, however, as a sudden enlightenment; a visionary experience. It is then particularly profound, blessed, and meaningful. Such a mystical experience may nevertheless "not be induced even by decade-long meditation," as Balthasar Staehelin writes. Also, it does not happen to everyone, although the capacity for mystical experience belongs to the essence of human spirituality.

Nevertheless, at Eleusis, the mystical vision, the healing, comforting experience, could be arranged in the prescribed place at the appointed time, for all of the multitudes who were initiated into the holy Mysteries. This could be accounted for by the fact that an hallucinogenic drug came into use; this, as already mentioned, is something that religious scholars believe.

The characteristic property of hallucinogens, to suspend the boundaries between the experiencing self and the outer world in an ecstatic, emotional experience, makes it possible with their help, and after suitable internal and external preparation, as it was accomplished in a perfect way at Eleusis, to evoke a mystical experience according to plan, so to speak.

Meditation is a preparation for the same goal that was aspired to and was attained in the Eleusinian

Mysteries. Accordingly it seems feasible that in the future, with the help of LSD, the mystical vision, crowning meditation, could be made accessible to an increasing number of practitioners of meditation.

I see the true importance of LSD in the possibility of providing material aid to meditation aimed at the mystical experience of a deeper, comprehensive reality. Such a use accords entirely with the essence and working character of LSD as a sacred drug.

CHEMICAL FORMULAS

Lysergic acid

Propanolamine

Diethylamine

Lysergic acid propanolamide

Ergobasin

Coramin

Lysergic acid diethylamide

LSD

Lysergic acid amide

Lysergic acid hydroxyethylamide

Active constituents of ololiuhqui

Psilocybin

Psilocin

Active constituents of teonanacatl

Serotonin
Neurohormone
Brain-active constituents